I KNOW HOW TO SET GOALS, SO WHY DON'T I ACHIEVE THEM?

I KNOW HOW TO SET GOALS, SO WHY DON'T I ACHIEVE THEM?

NICK HALL, PhD

MEDIA

MEDIA

Published 2019 by Gildan Media LLC
aka G&D Media
www.GandDmedia.com

FIRST EDITION 2019

Front Cover design by David Rheinhardt of Pyrographx

Interior design by Meghan Day Healey of Story Horse, LLC

Library of Congress Cataloging-in-Publication Data is available upon request

ISBN: 978-1-7225-0015-3

10   9   8   7   6   5   4   3   2   1

Contents

Introduction

I t was my third flat tire in less than two hours. Over two hundred pounds of kayak and gear far exceeded the weight capacity of the small trailer I was towing behind my folding bicycle. Three weeks earlier, I had set out from a gulf coast beach near St. Petersburg to circumnavigate the state of Florida. Now, with less than 400 miles remaining, I was about to drop out. My motivation-reserve had been used up during the course of multiple setbacks. I had set out on the 1,240 mile race, which included a 40 mile portage, three weeks earlier. On the first day while making very good progress down the Gulf of Mexico, I stopped to assist two competitors whose boat had capsized. They scrambled aboard my sailing kayak for a ride to the nearest beach, but the combination of extra weight and a rough surf damaged a critical part on the boat which had to be repaired before I could continue. I lost not only time, but also the winds that had been propelling me down the coast. Several days later while approaching the Florida Keys, I hit an oyster bar damaging yet another part of the boat. After a restless night, the tide eventually lifted me off the oyster bar so I could limp into Key Largo and make the necessary repairs. I wasn't really thinking about it, however, it did seem to take a greater amount of motivation to continue after the second mishap. Then, the mast broke a mile off shore while making good time up the Atlantic coast. Almost two days were lost while searching for the needed part and then waiting for the epoxy glue to cure. By now I was ready to pack it in, but somehow found the will to press on, although in my effort to make up lost time, I found myself in a severely sleep-deprived state. While approaching the entrance to the St. Mary's River on the Georgia border, I was capsized by a wave I didn't see in the darkness. More damage and more time was lost while making repairs. Still, I pressed on eventually arriving at the start of a 40 mile portage to the head waters of the Suwannee River. During the inaugural race in 2006, I had placed second in my division, in part by carrying a folding bike and small trailer in my decked canoe. I figured it would be a quick and efficient way to knock off the miles, which it proved to be in the first event. But in 2010, I was using a much heavier boat and had more gear. Although I was aware of the 150 pound capacity of the small trailer, I assumed the manufacturer was being overly cautious in setting the limit. But whatever the limit was, 230 pounds of boat and gear was too much. Depending upon which tire burst, I veered either into oncoming traffic or into the ditch. Neither was a pleasant, nor safe option. As the sun dropped below the trees, I decided it was not my year and dropped out.

Why, after three weeks and successfully covering nearly a thousand miles of rough seas, along with cold, wet conditions did I lose the motivation to continue? After all, the worst was over. All that remained was riding an ambling current the length of the Suwannee, then the relatively calm waters of the Gulf of Mexico back to the start.

The reason is because motivation is subject to the same type of fatigue that an athlete might experience during the running of a marathon. Depending upon training and the demands being placed on the muscles, if it exceeds the person's capacity for endurance, the muscles stop responding. Glucose is depleted and the will to continue disappears. It's called hitting the wall or bonking. In a similar way, the more you have to draw upon your motivation to pursue a goal, the greater the likelihood you will experience 'Motivation Fatigue'. You'll deplete your reserves in a manner similar to an athlete who bonks or hits the wall. In this audio book/program, I'll explain how you can build this motivation-reserve so you are less likely to lose the will to continue toward your goal. I'll describe a formula for setting goals, and how the way you define success can doom you to failure or propel you toward your goal. You'll also learn the characteristics of people who have overcome seemingly insurmountable odds to live their dreams, and the things you can do to acquire those same characteristics. However, a great deal of time will be devoted to exploring how your belief-shaped thoughts serve as the final determinant of success or failure, along with the ways you can increase your motivation-reserve in the same way you can increase your endurance for physical activities. Yes, through practice and careful training you can increase your will and thereby enjoy more success than you ever dreamed was possible.

But first, I'll introduce myself and explain why I am keenly interested in motivation and the things that influence it. I'm Nick Hall, and since I received a Ph.D in Neuroscience in 1976, I have conducted NIH and privately sponsored research delving into how the brain and emotions impact health and well-being. That research has been featured on CBS's 60-Minutes, the Emmy Award winning television series, Healing and the Mind, produced by Bill Moyers for PBS, and the BBC NOVA series. It's also a topic I speak about to doctors and nurses during continuing medical education seminars, and to corporate clients at my Saddlebrook Resort headquarters in Florida. There, I instruct elite athletes and leaders of some of America's top companies to achieve a state of optimal performance. In addition to having an understanding of the human brain and how it influences motivation, I also enjoy challenging pursuits like the Ultimate Florida Challenge, and cross-country bicycle trips. My first cycling trip was a nearly two-thousand mile ride from the Black Hills of South Dakota to Chicopee, Massachusetts. That journey was completed when I was 17. Fifty years later during the summer of 2015, I rode three thousand miles from Oceanside, California to St. Augustine, Florida. During those and many other adventures, I was able to draw upon my knowledge of the human brain to better understand my thoughts and choices when faced with adversity. I look forward to sharing those insights with you and thereby provide you with a greater awareness of why we often keep doing those things we shouldn't, and sometimes fail to do those we should. Most importantly, I'll describe the things you can do to achieve even what may at first appear to be the most elusive goal. You'll learn that sometimes the greatest obstacle to success is not the one you can see, but the one hidden in your own thoughts and beliefs.

Learn from Others

Why repeat the mistakes of others when there's an opportunity to learn from those who have gone before you? This is something I have been doing for most of my life, especially when I first left academia and decided to apply the knowledge I had acquired. My research had always focused upon how the brain and emotions impact health in the context of disease. In other words, why do people get sick and how can an understanding of the brain and immune system keep them healthy. It was important and necessary research delving into the biochemical pathways linking the brain and immune system. But one day while reflecting upon my research, I wondered about its relevance to the human condition. Eventually, I closed my research lab, and set off on a quest to discover the secrets of highly successful people. The journey began at LGE Sports Sciences where three friends, Jim Loehr, Pat Etcherberry, and Jack Groppel were advising elite athletes on ways to achieve the ideal performance state. My arrival added a medical component to the strategies being developed, and at the same time provided me with the opportunity to gain insights from people who had perfected the art of staying focused and summonsing the self-motivation to persevere despite physical and mental obstacles. Dan Jansen, the then world champion speed skater was one of many such athletes working with Jim Loehr and the LGE team. Later, I'll describe how he used the same approach professional actors use to eventually win an Olympic gold medal while setting an new world record. I eventually moved my headquarters to Saddlebrook Resort near Tampa, FL. Saddlebrook was designed to provide both athletes and corporations with an environment conducive to achieving success. Saddlebrook's clients have included the New York Yankees Derek Jeter, and tennis star John Isner. Corporate clients too numerous to list represent some of the worlds top corporations that have come celebrate their successes, or plot strategies for reaching future goals. Despite having different objectives, both the athletes and corporate clients share one thing in common; emerging victorious, whether it's on the sports field or corporate boardroom.

During the course of conversations with company presidents or CEO's, I'll pose a series of questions including, *"To what do you attribute your success? What advice would you offer to someone starting out? How do you cope with adversity?"* Many of these insights have come from members of the Worlds Presidents Organization. Membership is restricted to the leaders of companies with annual assets in excess of $240 million. Clearly, these are highly successful individuals from whom we can learn. Here is a brief summary of what they and others have shared:

1. You have to experience adversity in order to acquire effective coping skills.
2. Play the game to win, not to avoid losing.
3. Make sure the goal is something you want, not the expectation of someone else.
4. Learn from mistakes.
5. When set backs occur, recognize that some of the reasons were beyond your control. Don't personalize failure.
6. Don't be afraid of failure. It's an opportunity to learn.
7. Respect authority, but be willing to stand up to it.
8. Have the courage to press on, but the wisdom to stop when the cost is likely to be less than the reward.
9. Do not allow yourself to be defined by societies labels, especially those that impose limitations.
10. Learn by observing others.

Another way I've collected information is by surveying audiences. During the course of a highly successful speaking career, I've had the opportunity to interact with people from just about all walks of life. Doctors, FBI agents, corporate leaders, military personnel, and professional athletes. Teachers, labor unions, real estate agents and attorneys are others I have addressed amongst the diverse groups seeking to achieve success. I'll often ask the members of the audience to reflect upon someone they know who has it together. A person who views adversity not as an insurmountable obstacle, but as an opportunity to challenge themselves. I'll then ask them to call out the words they would use to characterize that person. Despite the wide diversity and different pursuits, those people who come to mind consistently share certain characteristics in common. They are relaxed and calm and relatively free of anxiety. They have a large amount of energy but it's positive energy. They are people who have a good sense of humor and they are fun to be with. They are enjoyable. They can do things with seemingly very little effort, almost automatically. As a consequence, they have a great deal of confidence. They are people who are alert. They are also in control, but by control I don't mean domineering. They are in control of their own emotions. And perhaps most important of all, they are focused. They can set their sites upon the objective and then if necessary reframe potentially negative emotions such as anger or fear, into a positive force.

Create Your Blueprint

Use the same process to determine the type of person you want to be. Take a moment to reflect for just a moment upon that one person in your life—a grandparent, parent, close friend, or, perhaps, a mentor—who always seems to make the right decision, no matter how much pressure they are under. Someone whose behavior you have tried to emulate when you've found yourself facing difficult circumstances. How would you describe this individual? What words come to mind that characterize this person to whom you look up? Chances are this person reflects your own beliefs and values and if you are like most people, the words that come to mind are likely balanced, controlled, confident, compassionate, caring, flexible, energized, calm, and peaceful. If these are the common characteristics of people you admire, then they are probably the characteristics that you most value and desire to have yourself. You can become that person. Let's look closely at that list again.

BALANCED

These are people who don't just talk the talk; they walk the walk. They have a good balance of work and family time. They eat well and exercise. They relax and play. They are involved in their communities. They have plenty of social interaction, yet they take the time to reflect and allow time for themselves. They live a balanced life. Most importantly, they conduct their lives in a manner that is consistent with their beliefs and values. They don't deviate. Their value system is like an old friend, a constant that keeps them centered, even during the most severe stress.

CONTROLLED

These are people who are in control. But, by control, I do not mean the ability to manipulate or to control other people. Instead, they are in control of their own emotions, and, as a result of not allowing anger, fear, or sadness to interfere with their objectives, they are able to remain focused.

CONFIDENT
They are people who are able to do things with seemingly very little effort and, as a consequence, they are, indeed, confident. In addition, they are able to instill confidence in others, which is why people often gravitate towards them. The best way to attain confidence is to gain knowledge. The more you know, the better you can predict. And the more accurate your predictions, the less you will fear.

COMPASSIONATE AND CARING
They are individuals who often engage in altruistic pursuits. They believe in the inherent good of all people. They do not prejudge others.

FLEXIBLE AND ENERGIZED
These are people who are active physically as well as mentally. They are open-minded people who gather as much information as they can so that their perception of the world is realistic.

CALM AND PEACEFUL
They have core beliefs that match their system of living. Their way of life reflects what they believe. They are in their optimal emotional state—that condition when the emotion they feel and express will help propel them

towards a worthwhile goal. They are healthy, and are working and living to their fullest potential. Chances are they will accomplish the ultimate goal of having maximum functional capacity right up until their final breath.

Chances are, this is a description of what you aspire to be like, not the way you are now. So what is preventing you from accessing this optimal state? First, think of the times you have been able to access this state. Everything seemed to flow easily; your thinking was clear, you performed flawlessly, and you accomplished more than expected; you were relaxed, and you felt good about yourself and what you were doing. You were in the zone or what Jim Loehr called the Ideal Performance State.

Maybe it happened on the golf course—one of those days when you just couldn't miss. Or the time you gave a presentation and pulled it off flawlessly. Or, wrote a paper effortlessly. Or, put together that new intergalactic spacecraft with your six-year-old. You hardly needed directions. Remember those times when you weren't anxious or frustrated. You were balanced, controlled, confident, compassionate, caring, flexible, energized, calm, and peaceful. What stops you from accessing this state more often? What prevents you from acquiring those qualities you most admire in your favorite person? I suspected it's an erroneous belief about your ability to accomplish goals? Here are some I often hear, and which, invariably, are not justified and thereby impede progress towards attaining a goal.

- I'm awkward in crowds.
- I never do well on exams.
- There's nothing I can do about it.
- It runs in my family.
- Failure is bad; I must always succeed.
- Stress is bad, and it should be avoided.
- I'm too old to change.
- I'm no good at relationships.
- Nice guys finish last.

Any of these sound familiar? Some beliefs may be very difficult to change—especially when they are cultural, as many are. Look at your workplace culture. Do you believe you have to work a tremendous amount of over-time to get ahead? Do you believe that if you tell colleagues you are taking off early to see your daughter in a play or to go out with your husband to celebrate your wedding anniversary, they won't take you seriously? I know work-places where it's considered a badge of courage to not take a vacation. People are proud of having stored up 100 or more vacation days. Others display million mile tags on their airline baggage. They think they are projecting to others a symbol of how important they are. To me, it says the time they spend on their work is out of proportion with time spent with family, with community, and with self. And I know they are not nearly as productive as they think they are. They are driven by some of the common beliefs of their culture, instead of their own value system.

For just a moment, project your mind in space and time to the future. I know this may sound a bit morbid, but imagine you are lying on your deathbed. In your hour of final reflection, do you think that you're going to wish that you'd spent more time at the office, or more time with your family while pursuing personal goals?

Picture this. There's a guy with his family in front of a sculpture at the Whitney Museum, and he takes out his cell phone to check in with work. Cut to a new scene: there's a woman having lunch with her mother at a lovely restaurant, but she has her notebook computer on the table, checking her e-mail. Almost all advertisements surrounding technology want you to believe that you can have more downtime because you can be connected with work while you relax. This is a contradiction. You need to unplug, unwind, and just relax when you have the opportunity. Enjoy nothing else but the art in the museum when you are there, sharing the experience with your family. And don't miss out on the great conversation over lunch with your mom. Be where you are. That's an important part of living a centered life. When your life is in balance, your access to the optimal emotional state is easy and effortless. And that's the state you need to be in if you want to achieve goals.

An interesting experiment was carried out by a group of scientists interested in how just the presence of technology could interfere with recovery and relaxation. They hiked into a remote wilderness, having left their computers and smart phones behind. Not until several days had passed were they able to truly relax. The well ingrained habit of constantly checking with the lab and monitoring events persisted despite the absence of technology, causing anxiety about what they were missing. Then, gradually the subconscious habits of checking e-mails and phone messages throughout the day gradually disappeared. But it took several days before the scientists could truly relax. No wonder so many people are in a constant state of stress. Even though they left the workplace, the scientists were never fully disconnected. At the subconscious level, there was no interlude away from workplace stressors. There was no recovery to counter stress, and as a consequence they were less likely to achieve goals. Like many people, they make the mistake of equating action with progress. They believe that unless they are connected with their work environment, they cannot achieve success. In actuality, if they fail to balance stress with recovery, and to get their life in balance, they will rarely achieve the state of optimal performance that will propel them to success.

Achieving Goals

n order to achieve goals, you must begin by removing, or at least minimizing, potential impediments to success. There are many, however, the most crippling are those that reside within your mind. Granted, changes in the economy, the actions of others, and unexpected obstacles can derail even the most worthy plans despite the best intentions. But they pale in comparison to the impact your thoughts have. That's because you don't respond to reality. You respond to a mental image of reality. At this moment, you are not responding to my words, the objects in the setting in which you find yourself, nor the ambient sounds in the background. Instead, you are responding to the electrochemical transduction of visual and auditory information into an image in your mind. It is the image that gives rise to emotion, which in turn will motivate you to approach or avoid. We tend to approach those things associated with positive emotions such as love and joy, and avoid those linked with negative emotions such as disgust and sadness. In addition, the image is driving the endocrine and autonomic nervous system pathways, which provide the biological foundation of the entire stress response. This is important to understand because it enables you to always have control over the impact events have upon your mental and physical well-being. You can't always control external events. But you can always exert a measure of control over your perception of those events.

Perception

No two people will perceive things in exactly the same way. Some people go to the airport on their day off, look forward to climbing aboard a perfectly functioning airplane, and then leap out of it at 10,000 feet as a member of their skydiving club. However, a person with a phobia of flying will see the air traffic control tower, observe the planes taking off and landing, and may have a full blown panic attack. Exact same stimulus. Totally different response. And clearly what is happening is in the perception. No two people will perceive things in the same way, and that is because they are never responding to absolute reality. What they are really responding to is an abstraction of reality as reflected in a mental image. Therefore, the image in your brain may be quite different from that of another person despite sharing the same experience. That's because your image will be shaped by past experience, your values and personal beliefs. As a result, two people hearing the same words may draw opposite conclusions about what was said.

I first came to this realization after presenting a seminar. Research I had conducted on the subject of guided imagery as a treatment for cancer had resulted in an interview with Diane Sawyer on the CBS television program *60 Minutes.* This national publicity resulted in numerous invitations from around the country to speak on this subject. As always, I presented a balanced viewpoint—speaking about the positive aspects of imagery and, at the same time, speaking about how it can hasten a person's demise depending upon their perceptions. At the end of the seminar, a lady came up to me and said, *"Dr. Hall, when I had cancer diagnosed, the doctors gave up on me. They said it was too advanced to respond to any of the available treatments and that I had less than 2 years to live. Then I read a book on imagery. It made sense so I tried it. Do you know that that was 6 years ago? I know the imagery saved my life, and I want to thank you for saying all the wonderful things you just said about it."* A short time later, a man came up and said, *"Dr. Hall, I'm a psychologist in Bethesda. I've always known that guided imagery is a crock, and I just want to tell you that it was very refreshing to hear a scientist who has done research in this area state it is a complete waste of people's time."* It was then that I understood the wisdom of the Chinese proverb, *"What the eye sees and what the ear hears is what is already in the mind."* In other words, we have a tendency to create images that will validate a pre-existing belief. It's analogous to the artist who is contemplating a beautiful scene. She sets up her easel, props up the canvas, and takes out her paints. And then she begins to assess the view and determine what to put down on that canvas. She soon realizes there must be an airport nearby because, periodically, planes fly across the horizon. But she decides the planes don't belong in this natural setting, so even though they are part of the reality, she doesn't include them. And behind her is a beautiful, weathered cedar tree, which is really not part of the scene. But how it would add to the painting if it were. So in her image, the tree is moved to the foreground. It's called artistic license, and we all do it. We have a tendency to delete those things that we do not want to be part of our image, and we include things in our image that were never a part of reality. In addition, the image changes over time as we have more experiences, and we get further and further from the actual event. The image becomes a less and less accurate abstraction of what actually happened. It is not that people are deliberately deceiving themselves. NO. They could pass a lie detector test with flying colors. The mind tends to operate on some sort of belief-driven autopilot. It's important to recognize that the initial event that gives rise to the emotion is not the image but rather the belief that shapes the information giving rise to that image. Thus, a mismatch between your belief and the circumstances may result in far more than a small amount of artistic license. Now, the image may become so distorted, it drives unhealthy emotions, which in turn greatly impair your ability to achieve goals.

Creating Mental Images

Up until now, I have discussed how your beliefs can shape images triggered by events around you. But do you know that you can create images based upon events within you? These images, in turn, can help you achieve the goals you dream of. It's a very effective way to interject a brief, recovery interlude into the chaotic environment you might find yourself in. It's something you can easily learn and as a result, experience a state of mind that will make achieving goals more likely.

First, determine what your image will be. Your favorite vacation spot. A quiet room. A concert hall, beach, or garden. It can be from your past and based upon fact, or it can be a creation of your imagination. Or, perhaps, you'd like to create a mental collage, drifting from one pleasant place to another. If it helps, gaze upon the scene in a picture, and let that be your setting, imagining that you are now a part of it.

Select an object, a fragrance, or a piece of music that will be a part of your image. Make it something unusual, something that you would not normally encounter. This is going to be your 'trigger.' By having it present when you create the image, it will acquire similar properties as Pavlov's bell. Except, you want it to activate the emotions and physiology associated with your imagery session. Later, just by exposing yourself to the trigger, you will more quickly enter the state you want to be in.

Isolate yourself from distracting, sensory stimuli. Make sure the room is quiet, that you are comfortable, and there are no distractions. Include dimensions that will enhance your image. Appropriate music and fragrances may enrich the mood, so let them bath your imagination.

Relax. If your mind is preoccupied with something else, intrusive thoughts will make it difficult for you to create anything except superficial images. Colors, aromas, sounds, and an awareness of small details within the place you have created will only transpire when you are totally relaxed. Take a warm bath. Listen to relaxing music. Read some poetry. Take deep, abdominal breaths. Use progressive muscle relaxation. Do whatever works for you.

Immerse yourself in your journey. Picture the setting from afar, as though you are watching the scene on a large, theater screen. Observe the objects, people, sounds, fragrances, and colors. Is it warm or cold? Identify a place where you would like to be, and move towards it, noting how everything changes with your perspective. Become a part of the scene. Create a scene that warrants a smile. As you take in your surroundings, gently rotate your head in a tension-releasing sweep around your shoulders, observing new things as your head slowly moves.

Practice creating images. Remember, it's your belief-driven image that governs the emotions, which, in turn, are able to impact every aspect of your personal and professional life. If you want to experience success in reaching your goals, you must learn to control your images.

The more open-minded you are, the more you read, the more you experience, the more feedback you accept from other people, the more willing you are to listen to alternative viewpoints, then the more information that will go into your image, and the greater the probability that your image will more closely reflect reality. While perception creates the image, beliefs shape the perception. And that's the part you can change. To determine if your belief is appropriate for the circumstances, examine your beliefs, not just the circumstances. And then by simply reframing the belief, you may well transform it into a catalyst for success, not failure. For example, instead of concluding, *"I can't possibly do this"*, you can say, *"I cannot do this right now, but, perhaps, if I take classes on the subject, I will acquire the skills I need to achieve this objective."* And remember to examine where the belief came from. Is it your's or someone elses? I wonder how many gifted athletes, scientists, and artists are unknown to the world because of a chance statement by a parent or friend proclaiming, *"Oh, you can't possibly make a living doing that,"* *"or you're not coordinated enough to play sports"* and they never even pursued their dream. People who achieve great success challenge beliefs that might hold them back. For example, an African-American girl born into poverty in a small, Southern town in Mississippi, who, at the age of 13, suffered abuse and molestation and became a runaway teenager. What are the chances of her becoming a successful woman who reaches out and helps millions of people every day? What if Oprah Winfrey had created beliefs reflecting failure instead of ones spelling success?

Could you have imagined a college dropout who went to Albuquerque, New Mexico, to follow his preposterous dream, who began his business in a cheap motel with hookers next door, would end up the richest man in the world? No erroneous belief stopped Bill Gates. And who would have thought a gal born in Nutley, New Jersey—a former model turned caterer—would start a homemaking business and become an entrepreneur who could rival the likes of Bill Gates? Nothing –not bad advice nor criticism—stopped Martha Stewart from achieving her goals. And, thank goodness, Michael Jordan did not accept the belief of his high school basketball coach in Wilmington, North Carolina. The coach who told him that he was not good enough to play basketball. How fortunate that Michael Jordan didn't allow this erroneous belief to keep him from pursuing his goal. Many people confronted with the same circumstances these highly successful people faced may well have simply accepted their lot in life and never attempted to set goals to improve themselves. The difference? Those who succeed form beliefs that instill a sense of optimism they can succeed. They have confidence and when inevitable setbacks occur, they continue to believe in their own abilities and remain optimistic. Make sure that you know what your beliefs are. It's the most important step. Many people don't know. Then determine if your belief is based on accurate and complete information.

Sometimes we tend to formulate a belief based on only a fragment of the information available to us. Perhaps I should mention that I happen to be clairvoyant and can peer into the future. I can tell you right now who will be the nominees in the next American presidential election. There will be a Democrat, a Republican, and an Independent party candidate. And I know a lot about these candidates, much of which will not be known publicly until after the election. These will be your choices. Candidate number one is a chain smoker, drinks half a dozen martinis throughout the day, and has had two elicit sexual affairs. Candidate number two is also a chain smoker; he sleeps until noon, admits to having smoked opium in college, drinks champagne during the afternoon, and sometimes knocks off a quart of brandy in the evening before going to bed. Candidate number three is a decorated war hero, champions the cause of the common man, drinks an occasional beer, does not smoke, and has not had an illicit sexual affair. Would you be inclined to vote for candidate number one, candidate number two, or candidate number three? Candidate number one was Franklin Roosevelt. Candidate number two, Sir Winston Churchill. And candidate number three, Adolph Hitler.

Sometimes, we have a tendency to make decisions and to formulate a belief based upon only a fragment of the information available to us. And that belief is shaped, in part, by our value system. Some people value certain things so profoundly that unless the person they work with subscribes to exactly the same religion or has exactly the same health habits, they will make no attempt to even meet that individual, when, in fact, that person might enable them to achieve new heights in their profession. Or your neighbor down the street might be your new, potentially best, friend. But because of one characteristic, you may make no attempt to even meet that person. Occasionally, your intuition pays off, and you should reject a person based upon a tiny fragment of information. More often, however, the greater the amount of information you acquire, the more options you will have in making an informed decision capable of getting you closer to that elusive goal.

Role of Beliefs

While the image you respond to is informed by external events and the actions of others, you always exert ultimate control through experiences, values, and beliefs. Past experiences represent water under the bridge. You can't go back in time and rewrite history, although you can decide what in your past you choose to focus upon. In that respect, you can draw upon past experiences to shape your image in either a negative or positive way. Therefore, the past can be modulated in a small way to influence your current thinking. So can values, although they are unlikely to change. If you are not making progress toward a goal, or simply can't get started on the path to success, it's best to examine the beliefs that may be holding you back. Here are some examples I heard when working with a large hospital that asked me to develop a wellness program that would improve the health of their employees. I'm including them because it's a failure to achieve health related goals that impacts the lives of many people. In addition, if you are not healthy, it will be difficult to achieve most any goal, including those at work. Here are the wellness related beliefs I heard described:

- Healthy eating is too expensive.
- I don't need to exercise; I walk all day at work.
- I have a low metabolism so I can't lose weight.
- I am under too much stress at work.
- My family cooks all the foods, and I can't refuse what I'm served.
- I don't know what healthy choices are.
- I can't stick to a strict diet.
- I live in a dangerous neighborhood so I can't go outdoors and exercise.
- I lost the list of foods I need to stay away from.
- I don't like any of the foods that are good for me.
- With the holidays, it is impossible to stick to my routine.
- I'm not the one who buys the groceries.
- I have too many other health problems.
- It is too late. I'm too old.
- I've tried every kind of exercise and diet. Nothing works.
- I just take extra insulin if I eat too much.
- My doctor never tells me that I have to lose weight.
- My scales are broken.
- My exercise bike needs a new pedal.
- I'm hungry all the time.
- I'm bored, and I eat all day long.
- It's too painful to exercise.
- It's inconvenient.
- I don't have time.
- It's boring.

- It's hard to keep up.
- I'm too out of shape.

These listed reasons/excuses can be organized into 6 distinct categories that apply to the achievement of virtually any goal:

- Lack of time (I'm too busy.)
- Lack of money (Eating healthy is too expensive.)
- Lack of knowledge (I don't know what healthy choices are.)
- Lack of ability (I have too much pain to exercise.)
- Lack of motivation (I know what to do. I just don't do it.)
- Lack of optimism (It is too late, and I'm too old to change.)

Upon further inspection, this list of 6 distinct types of excuses corresponds to the 3 major constituents of a person: Mind, Body, and Spirit.

Mind: Insufficient knowledge is a function of the mind. So is lack of time, of which you have plenty. The problem is how you prioritize what you do with what's available.

Body: Having a multitude of health problems can represent a formidable obstacle. While it doesn't cause disease, stress can create an environment within the body making it easier for the causes of disease to rear their ugly heads. Stress can also sap your motivation to pursue goals.

Spirit: Lacking the will to change can be an insurmountable obstacle if not dealt with. So is a feeling of pessimism. Chances are, the real obstacle is the belief 'you can't do something' that's holding you back.

Some of these explanations are legitimate. It's difficult to engage in healthy pursuits when you're struggling to make it one day at a time. However, others are merely excuses for doing nothing. So how can you know which is which? By taking the following Belief Challenge Test.

Changing Unhealthy Beliefs

Whenever you encounter a belief—whether it's a core belief, a cultural belief, a hand-me-down belief, or an advertised belief—ask yourself, and then answer, these questions. I'm going to pose them in the context of how they affect your relationship with yourself, your family, your business associates, your neighbors, as well as the community-at-large. And dig deep for the answers. Plan to spend considerable time reflecting upon each. And don't assume that whatever first comes to mind is the only answer. Here they are:

- Are these your beliefs or those of someone else?
- Are your beliefs based upon experience?
- Can you think of times in your life when your belief was challenged by reality?
- Have your beliefs ever kept you from achieving a goal?
- Are certain themes reflected in your beliefs?

- Are you willing to change one or more of your beliefs if they impede the achievement of your goals?
- Are your beliefs serving a useful purpose?

My entire life has been shaped by another person's erroneous belief. I was 6 years old and in a state of emotional shambles when I learned I had failed an arithmetic exam. My mother, a wonderful lady, tried to console me. "Don't worry. No one in our family has ever done well in math. I'm sure you'll soon discover something you're good at." It made me feel a lot better. After all, it was not my fault. It was the fault of some distant ancestor who had passed on a faulty genetic blueprint that didn't include numbers. From that moment, I stopped applying myself in math classes. Why waste time and energy struggling to master a subject I was doomed to fail anyway. Instead, I applied myself to those subjects that did come readily. As long as I got a passing math grade and could move to the next level, I was quite content. It wasn't until more than a decade later when I was in graduate school that I realized my belief was wrong. It was while taking a class in statistics that I came to realize, not only is math not difficult, with a good instructor it can be quite interesting. Of course I also had a powerful incentive to master the subject. After all, I would need that tool to analyze the data I would be gathering in my chosen profession as a scientist. But how I've wondered how different my life might be had it not been for that one, well intended but erroneous statement. I might have become an accountant or chosen engineering as a pursuit instead of studying the brain and ways behavior can impact health and performance.

Begin the process right now by identifying a belief you would like to change. Pick one that is holding you back. Here's an example: *Better safe than sorry.* People are afraid of failure so they play it safe in both their personal and professional lives. You must overcome this belief if you are to be successful. Any change requires moving away from familiar territory. And any learning experience carries with it the risk of losing face. No wonder people stay where they are. Even though their business venture could have the potential of doubling its profits, or they might unleash the means to spend more time with their family by doing what they really want to do; instead, they remain in the same rut. We hold on to a belief because we have become set in our ways, and we resist change. We may want to do things differently, but we are afraid of failing. So instead of taking steps to improve our lot, we keep things status quo. We even create new beliefs to justify the rut we're in.

I have a friend who services clients for a large company. His job requires that he log nearly 50,000 miles a year driving throughout the Eastern USA. Every hour that he is on the road, he is away from his family and those things that bring pleasure. He was recently offered a promotion that would keep him at company headquarters close to home. *"No way,"* he told me. *"I'm not going to become part of that rat-race. Too much backbiting at headquarters. I'd rather be on my own, even if it means a lower salary and eating in truck stops."* Where does this belief come from? Perhaps from his early childhood. Many men are taught that they must be decisive and always make the right decision. Role models may have been present in the family or depicted on the television screen by childhood heroes. Or perhaps through the pages of books read to us by parents. Subtle messages conveying what a hero can and should be were present throughout our early upbringing. What happens, though, when the child encounters failure and realizes that success is not guaranteed? Then the fear of failure may result in that person becoming indecisive or avoiding situations requiring that he or she take charge and accept responsibility. The person might seek employment in a subservient position so someone else can shoulder the responsibility for failure. Not only will this belief impact the person's professional life, but they may also seek a spouse who plays a dominant role in their relationship. Achieving any goal will be almost impossible in the shadow of such beliefs.

While in some cases it might be necessary to consult with a therapist to help with the process, by asking the right questions, you can usually identify for yourself what is triggering a particular behavioral path. Often, just understanding the basic mechanism of what is going on and coming to grips with what the initiating event might be is all that it takes to initiate the first step toward change.

Remember, images gives rise to responses including emotions. The root of the word 'emotion' is the same one that gave rise to the word, 'motivate'. Therefore, experiencing the appropriate emotion that will motivate you to achieve a goal is essential. But many people have difficulty appraising their emotions, even when appropriate. Perhaps your inability to experience certain emotions is because of how or whether you were accepted by your family or social group as a child. Emotions often will be denied when they are seen as unacceptable to others. Consequently, you may repress an emotion through fear of rejection. A fear that originated decades ago when you weren't even old enough to remotely understand the process, now shapes your decisions as an adult. Healthy people are able to acknowledge appropriately expressed anger, envy, or sexual feelings without imposing punishment. People feel free to discuss not only their own emotions, but to be available to others who need to express their own. A person who has been raised in this type of open environment is more likely to take responsibility for their feelings and not to blame others for how they feel. As a consequence, they will be more comfortable with other people, and with making decisions; decisions that must be made to achieve success.

There are things you can do to overcome obstructive beliefs. Begin by asking the Belief Challenge questions I reviewed earlier. You are the only one who can answer these questions. Write them down, and then read the answers out loud. Sometimes, when you receive information via multiple sensory modalities, it's easier to process and to understand. Consider all the sources of beliefs that I mentioned earlier. When asking if a given belief is justified, reflect upon previous occasions when that belief influenced your behavior. What was the outcome? Even if you weren't successful, was the outcome really all that bad? Bad enough to prompt you never again to attempt to move forward? And while you are at it, which decisions do you most regret? Those you made or those you didn't? Then list all of the ways your life may change if you accept the challenge of changing your belief and succeed? Remember, there is no single correct answer to any of these questions. But take the time to answer them. Collect as much information as possible. Perhaps the cost/benefit ratio will not be worth it. And that's okay. Or perhaps you should chance it. That's okay, too. You must decide on the basis of your beliefs, and the goals which they may impact.

Let's return to the notion that it is a mismatch between your belief and the environment, which leads to failure. You always have two choices. When you have a mismatch, you have the choice of changing the environment to match your belief or changing your belief to match the environment. Some people have a tendency to do one or the other consistently. People who are centered tend to view the world the way it really is, instead of living in a dreamlike fantasy fueled by erroneous beliefs. People who are realistic about what they want, know how to go about getting it. These people are open-minded individuals, who will gather as much information as possible, and then they are willing to adjust their beliefs if they realize those beliefs no longer have value. In contrast are the close-minded people. These individuals try to limit the amount of information that they will listen to, and they will walk away from any discussion of a belief counter to their own. Such people are constantly trying to persuade others of the validity of their religious or political viewpoints, without acknowledging any other interpretation. These are the people who are invariably going to experience emotions that are negative and which in turn will trigger avoidance. That's not where you want to be during the pursuit of a goal.

But you always have an option. You can change your belief, or you can try to change the environment. Sometimes you have to change the environment. If you are being asked in the work place to do something that is dishonest or otherwise counter to your belief, it clearly is a good idea to change the environment and to get another job. Or perhaps your marriage has become so destructive to the well-being of you and your family that divorce is the only sensible option. That may be a very difficult decision. A bad relationship can be difficult to abandon because you may have a guilt-driven compulsion to keep returning to try to make it work. Such futile efforts may be driven by a belief that 'giving up is always bad.' Or they may result from an unwillingness to initiate change because, despite the turmoil, you are at least familiar with the status quo.

Of course, there are times when your beliefs are simply not correct. You don't have enough information, or you are focusing on the wrong type of information, in which case it probably is better to change your image of reality. And, there are situations where it isn't exclusively a problem of the environment nor of your beliefs. You may not be able to leave a job in its entirety, but there may be things you can do to modify the environment and to partially modify your beliefs and perceptions so the match is sufficiently close so that you can achieve a higher level of emotional well-being. Still, you always have an option. The option of changing your environment or of changing your belief—or a little bit of both. *"Is my belief justified?"* You have to ask this question in every situation. The belief that a firm and swift punishment is beneficial may be justified when teaching your children the difference between right and wrong. But that same belief may be totally inappropriate in the office where you may want to encourage others to take the risks required to achieve a new level of profitability.

Beliefs and Personal Goals

've been focusing upon beliefs that prevent us from achieving professional goals. However, there are additional ones that can have a profound effect upon personal relationships. These are ones based upon biases or faulty perceptions that interfere with growth and personal happiness, regardless of the environment. Often these beliefs are learned during childhood and are reinforced throughout life. We know intellectually that these perspectives are faulty, but we have difficulty changing due to the strong emotions associated with the belief. Often these beliefs are so ingrained that we use them without thinking, despite the fact that they can lead to feelings of sadness, hopelessness, fear, or anxiety; emotions that will spill over and interfere with the attainment of just about any goal. The following are ten common beliefs with which many people struggle. As you review them, ask yourself which of these 10 beliefs may operate consciously or unconsciously in your life.

1. *I must be loved, validated, and approved by everyone.* This belief keeps you from being yourself for fear that you will meet with disapproval or rejection. Individuals who subscribe to this belief often cheat themselves out of being who they are, focusing instead on evaluating situations and other people for how to respond. As a result, difficulties in both professional and personal relationships are common due to the fact that a healthy relationship requires two separate individuals who respect their own and each other's identity.

2. *I am responsible for other people.* By taking responsibility for others, you may inadvertently take away their motivation to accept responsibility for themselves. In addition, you put yourself in a no-win situation. Controlling other people is rarely, if ever, possible. When you do this, you lose touch with yourself. How do people get this way? They often come from families where everyone made unreasonable demands or were possessive of others. They have little respect for another person's individual identity because they never learned what it means. Instead of being open and soliciting dialogue, they attempt to read other people's minds and probe into their affairs, believing they have every right to do so. They can't see the boundary between where their self ends and an-

other's begins. They have a very precarious sense of their own identity.

3. *My happiness depends on people and on things outside of myself.* Many people try to achieve inner happiness through other people or other things. While other people or things may provide you with some temporary comfort or pleasure, they cannot provide lasting happiness. Ultimately, your happiness depends on you. It's not that simple, though. You need to be flexible and to adapt to the circumstances. Basically, when things are going well, you want to have a strong sense of being involved and of being a part of the process. This is something that psychologists refer to as an internal locus of control. But when things are going badly, you need to step out of that role. Give it your best shot, but recognize there are some things you simply cannot control, such as another person's behavior. Sometimes, a sense of external locus of control can be beneficial. A healthy response is being able to say, *"I did all that I could, but, ultimately, the decision was made by someone I couldn't influence."* When you don't even try, it may be because you attribute whatever happens in your life to outside factors.

4. *I must be the best at everything I do—I can't make mistakes.* Perfectionism is a battle that many people fight every day. It is important to accept that

everybody has areas of strength and weakness—to be human is to be imperfect. While everybody likes to excel, no one can possibly excel at everything. Most successful people have succeeded only after many failures or mistakes. Life is a learning experience. Some people cannot acknowledge an imperfection because they never received the love and support to feel comfortable with their shortcomings. Deep down, they feel like worthless human beings, and they end up making unreasonable demands upon themselves and, sometimes, on others. In that unrealistic, over demanding world, they are able to justify their belief that they are hopeless because their self-imposed demands are so unrealistic. In order to feel good about themselves, they will project their faults onto other individuals or groups, and blame them for whatever goes wrong. In short, when they criticize others, they are really revealing their own shortcomings.

"She rises at 6:00am, meditates for half an hour, wakes up her 2.3 kids, feeds them a grade A nutritious breakfast (which they eat), sends them off to school, puts on a $600 Anne Klein suit, goes to her $125,000 job, which is creative and socially useful, runs six miles on her lunch break, spends a wonderful hour of genuine, quality time with her children after school, then cooks a gourmet meal in her spotless designer kitchen. While cooking dinner, she discusses economic trends with her husband, and then, during family mealtime, continues to relate to her

husband and children about meaningful topics. After the children are tucked in bed, she spends more quality time with her husband, and ends the evening with several hours of passionate lovemaking with multiple orgasms. She then has a good night's sleep, and in the morning she wakes refreshed and eager to start all over again."

Obviously, if you believe each day should resemble this description of Superwoman penned by the newspaper columnist, Ellen Goodman, you are going to have very low self-esteem as you constantly fail to achieve this unrealistic standard. By the way, perfectionism is okay in some environments. It's good that engineers at NASA are perfectionists. And you want your surgeon to adhere to the highest standards imaginable. You just need to distinguish between standards that are warranted and those that are unreasonable.

5. *I can avoid dealing with problems or pain in life.* While you can postpone addressing difficulties and discomfort, you cannot completely avoid tough times indefinitely. Accepting them and dealing with problems and emotions directly allows you to put them behind you. Avoiding emotions is rarely effective for the long term. It is not possible to fully enjoy positive feelings when you have denied negative feelings. It is the failure to acknowledge an emotion that will wreak havoc in your life. I'm not suggesting that you walk into

your boss' office and engage in a form of emotional exhibitionism. Carefully chose the right time and place. Remember, the emotion is signaling a perceived unmet need or problem that needs to be addressed. Denying the emotion is ignoring the problem. You have a choice. You can deal with it consciously on your terms, or you can wait for it to surprise you when your body can't take it anymore.

6. *Inconveniences in life are catastrophes.* It is important to keep the daily hassles and inconveniences in life in proper perspective. What is the worst-case scenario? Is it really as bad as you fear? Life is full of problems. Your choice is whether or not you accept this fact or repeatedly set yourself up for disappointment by expecting life to be hassle-free. Paradoxically, when you accept this fact, the hassles become easier to tolerate.

7. *I must be in control at all times.* It is a fact that there are many things in life beyond our control. However, we are consistently in control of our attitude, and our happiness. If we believe in the illusion of control, we will repeatedly face the impossible task of trying to govern what is beyond us. While it is beneficial to maintain control over situations that we can influence, the belief that we have power over all events is an illusion that is responsible for much unhappiness. As I noted previ-

ously, it's good to have control over some things. Problems arise when control becomes the end instead of the means, when we refuse to relinquish it even when circumstances call for delegation or simply letting go. Reinhold Niebuhr said it best: *"God, grant me the serenity to accept the things I cannot change, courage to change the things I can, and wisdom to know the difference."*

8. *If people knew the real me, they would not like me.* This belief can cause you to pretend to be someone you are not, ultimately distancing yourself from other people, including those people who might truly appreciate and enjoy the person you really are. The bad news is that you probably do have some traits or features that others might consider undesirable. The good news is, everyone does. Furthermore, when you can see your own limitations, it becomes easier to accept those of others. You'll be more realistic and not expect people to be better than they really are. There will be other benefits as well. You'll have less of a tendency to exaggerate the negative.

9. *It is wrong to enjoy myself too much.* While life is sometimes painful and difficult, it is healthy to enjoy life and to make a decision to seek fulfillment and joy out of the experiences available to you. Once you accept this, you become closer to and appreciate more the people around you.

10. *I can't change because I've always been the way that I am.* If you truly believe this, it's likely you have sealed yourself off. Choices are made each and every moment in life. While making changes is sometimes very difficult, you effect change simply by making choices. What characterizes truly healthy people is having the capacity to deal with change. Often, they thrive on it as they view events not as obstacles but as challenges. Many people can't seem to maintain openness and flexibility, and they end up distraught when things don't turn out as they expected. For these people, even minor changes can make them feel overwhelmed. Realize that when you achieve a goal, there likely will be changes. Some are known and anticipated. Others may be more subtle and not apparent until you achieve your success. The inability to accept this change may result in the unraveling of your initial success.

These ten beliefs can interfere not only with your professional development, but also your personal enrichment. They will keep you from achieving your goals by giving rise to unhealthy emotions and by extension, inappropriate responses.

Who Are You?
How Do You View Life?

Who are you? When you introduce yourself to someone and have to give a one or two sentence explanation of who you are, how do you answer? Like this? *"Hi. I'm Nick Hall, Director of Important Stuff at the XYZ Corporation."* Is your identity attached to your work? If so, you might have too much of your self-esteem, of who you are as a person, tied to the workplace. If one day you awaken, and you are not Nick Hall, Director of Important Stuff at the XYZ Corporation, who would you be? What would you be if you lost your job tomorrow—and I'm not talking about the financial implications? If you lost your job tomorrow, how would you define yourself? You could no longer say, "I'm Director of Important Stuff." You could no longer say, "I work at the XYZ Corporation." Are you a daughter, a brother, a mother, a son? Are you a sailor, a gardener, a seamstress, a wood worker, an artist? Your personal identity will, in turn, shape your beliefs. If your beliefs are enabling you to make progress toward achieving your goals, I suspect the emotions you experience are largely positive and fulfilling. But, if your beliefs are keeping you from achieving your goals, you probably are experiencing many negative emotions. And, if you don't know what your beliefs or goals are, then you probably bounce from one emotional state to another without knowing why.

Why is it that some people live life so passionately and so fully? They work at jobs they love. They enjoy their family. They have mastered the art of pleasure, and they are rich in every aspect of their life because they are living to their fullest potential. Could it be as simple as the fact that their system for living truly reflects their core beliefs and values? I think so.

Discovering What You Value

As I lecture around the country on beliefs, emotions, stress, and related mind/body issues, I find that most people don't really believe they can be whatever they want to be, or that they can do whatever it is they want to do. Their beliefs won't allow them to accept this. I find, too, that most people don't really value what they are currently doing, and they don't really value what they have or could have. And it's not for lack of trying. Do you know people who go to seminar after seminar? Who read self-help books and obediently complete audio programs, but they still can't seem to put it all together to make the necessary changes? Do you know someone like that? Even if they get a better job, they are still not happy. Oh, they might be happy for a little while, but the same problems seem to resurface at work and at home and with money. And then what happens? They get angry, afraid, depressed, or ashamed. Their actions, the way they live, the jobs they work at, are not congruent with their core beliefs. And because their beliefs are in conflict with their lifestyle, it affects their emotional state in ways that are highly detrimental to their physical and mental health. It affects how they feel about themselves, the way they eat, whether or not they exercise, what they do for a living, the quality of their family life, and how they plan for the future.

So, how do you know who you are and what you really believe is important? Here's a fun way to find out what's near and dear to you. Imagine that you have just opened the door; standing there is a representative from a lottery with a check for 10 million dollars. But, there's a catch. You have 5 minutes to decide what to do with it—every last penny. And what you don't account for, you don't get. Start writing; and remember, you have only 5 minutes. What immediately comes to mind? New house, new car, new clothes? Many people go directly to advertised beliefs, including what they believe success should look like, or, more likely, what they have been told being rich looks like. Be careful. You may be spending your money and redesigning your life based on somebody else's values. What about buying all those things for someone else? A mansion for your parents, a Mercedes for your best friend, a sport fishing boat for your brother-in-law, and two first class tickets on a cruise boat for a couple of friends? What's up with the big spender? Just being a nice person? Look closer. It could very well be a hand-me-down belief. Maybe you think you don't deserve the money, and you need to give it away. Or you've heard that rich people aren't nice; they're miserly, and so you give it away instead of becoming like that. Or, maybe, as a child, you never had enough money, so you're going to spend everything you have to show people that you now have it. And then what happens is that you end up with nothing again.

Look at your lottery list. Is a charitable organization mentioned? Or, did you immediately invest it all to make more money? What does this say about your values? Think carefully. Do you really need the purchases, or are you spending or not spending money in a way that is expected of you? What if you are unable to develop a list for all of this money? You have no idea what to do with it? Then you may not know what your core beliefs are, and you are going to have to dig a little deeper. Don't mistake the objective of this exercise. The intent is not to instill a particular belief—it's just to get you thinking about your own. There is no right or wrong belief. It's only when a belief is not justified for your circumstances or when it impedes your progress towards a worthwhile goal that it needs to be changed. Here are some incomplete sentences. Take a break, and finish the statement in a manner consistent with your beliefs and values.

Life is _____. A cynic might answer *a terminal disease.* A more positive response might be *a precious gift.*

*The world would be a better place to live if*_____. *There were no illnesses?* How about, *There were more goodwill.*

And here's one more example, which gets to the core of this process. *I am* _____.

Are you still uncertain about what it is you value? It goes hand in hand with your beliefs. Do you value money? power? labor? a higher power? Or, perhaps, family, your career, or material possessions? It matters less what you value. It does matter that you know what it is that you value.

Setting Goals

Now that you have identified your beliefs and your value system, what do you want to do with them? What do you want out of life? Many people live their entire life without ever asking this question, and, as a consequence, they fail to extract from life all that they might have had. A childhood prayer concludes: . . . *if I should die before I wake, I pray the Lord my soul to take.* A sad thought. Just as sad would be the substitution of the words: . . . *if I should die before I live.* Too many people drift aimlessly through life without a clear understanding of what they truly want. They eventually die at a ripe, old age, but they die before they have lived. More than likely, they never had any meaningful goals. Don't let this happen to you. Identify your personal goals now. Complete these statements, and do so on a regular basis, so that you don't forget.

1. In my lifetime, I want to _____.
2. Prior to retirement, I want to _____.

3. Before my children have left home, I want to

_____.

4. By _____, I want to _____.

Now ask yourself these questions:
- Are these goals attainable?
- Are they my goals or those of someone else?
- Are they stated concisely and as a positive objective?
- Am I willing to begin now? If not, under what circumstances will I begin?
- Am I willing to make changes in my life to achieve my goals?
- Are my goals consistent with my values and beliefs?
- Do any of my goals conflict with each other?
- What am I willing to give up to achieve my goals?

Establishing unrealistic goals is a sure way to experience failure. It's important to set goals for yourself. It's your life. Do what feels right for you, not what you think is expected of you by associates or by family members. You also must make a commitment to achieve your goals. Many people get involved in various projects that they believe will help them reach their objective, but they fail to get there because they don't make a commitment. True commitment means making sacrifices and delaying gratification. Establishing unrealistic goals is an effort in futility. And identifying goals that are inconsistent with your values and beliefs will be a constant source of conflict.

Over the years, while teaching in medical schools, I have encountered students who admitted they did not want to be doctors. When I asked why they pursued a career that was not to their liking, they invariably responded by explaining they had embraced someone else's belief. One young lady still stands out. She was a brilliant pianist who had chosen medical school over the opportunity to attend the Juliard School of Music on a scholarship. When I inquired why she would turn down such a rare offer, she explained that her parents and friends had told her she should view playing the piano as a hobby, not a profession. Eventually, she became convinced she couldn't make a decent living playing the piano and so pursued medicine instead. It was a decision she lived to regret. Mastering the medical subjects did not come easy for her, and when she stopped by my office, was worried she might fail the course. When I suggested she drop out of school and pursue her passion, she explained that even in her second year of medical school she already had accumulated a sizable debt and that she would have to become a physician to earn enough money to eventually pay off her student loans. How sad that the sense of regret would always be with her. And I'm sure that whenever she heard piano music or experienced some other reminder of her lost opportunity, this resulted in a feeling of sadness for which there would be no remedy.

Divide Your Goal into Achievable Sub-Goals

On July 13th, 2015, I set out on my bicycle from the town of Oceanside, CA to St. Augustine FL. It was an unsupported ride, which meant I was alone with everything I would need for the month long journey attached to my 1960's era ten speed bicycle. When I pushed down on the pedal after ceremoniously dipping my back tire in the Pacific Ocean, my definition of success was not to arrive in St. Augustine. It was going to take a month or more to complete the more the 3,000 mile journey and that was too long to wait for the satisfaction of having accomplished my goal. Nor was it to maintain a certain speed or to complete a set number of miles each day. Head winds, mechanical failures, and physical injury were the categories within which numerous things I had little if any control over could impact the distance I might cover on any particular day. No, my success was always defined by something I had complete control over, and which would provide me with continuous feedback regarding my progress. It was to make forward progress toward St. Augustine 15 hours per day. It was a realistic objective because it was the amount of daily sunshine I would likely have available. In addition, each time I glanced at my watch, I could take satisfaction in knowing I had made measurable progress. Of course I wanted eventually to arrive in St. Augustine and dip my front wheel into the Atlantic Ocean. However,achieving that milestone was not part of my definition of success; it was the reward I would reap for having completed each daily goal. Defining success in a way you have total control over is the first and most important step to achieving a goal. It didn't matter that my pace was barely a crawl ascending steep mountain passes, or battling strong headwinds. As long as I was moving in an easterly direction, I was successful. Industrial psychologists have studied job satisfaction and without fail, getting feedback about how well you are doing is one of the more important ways to experience it as you work to achieve professional goals. So, doesn't it make sense that defining success in a way that you get constant feedback will keep you motivated as you work toward your personal goal? And why not define success in a way that at the end of the day you will always have a measure of your success? This is important to do to avoid the one emotion that more than any other will interfere with your achieving goals. That emotion is fear of failure.

Use Your Time Wisely

suffer from a chronic condition, which keeps me in a constant state of turmoil. It's called Optimistic Bias, and it's characterized by the belief that *I can accomplish more than is humanly possible in a given amount of time.* If you suffer from the same malady, here are some things you might try. Many books have been written on the subject of how to manage your time, and there are numerous seminars that can help you get motivated. In general, the advice is basically the same: you need to have an idea of what needs to be accomplished in a given period of time, and then you need to set priorities. Everyone needs to have objectives that they want to achieve in order to give meaning to their life. Whatever the dream happens to be, it has to be realistic and something you truly want— not something you are doing just to please other people. Did you know that just thinking about a goal or writing that goal down will help facilitate your accomplishing it? Once you've identified what it is you want to achieve, it becomes easier to identify the information and circumstances that will help you achieve that success. Here are the ground rules:

Divide Projects into Manageable Components: Break your goal into smaller and more manageable component parts. The reason is quite simple. When you focus upon the endpoint, it may seem as though the project is overwhelming. If you want to write a book, it may be very difficult getting the motivation to begin because you feel that you couldn't possibly accomplish such a goal. But no one has ever written a book. Instead, people write words, which come together as sentences, which come together as paragraphs, which, in turn, become chapters. It's also a way to organize your time in the most efficient way possible.

Don't Always Set Time Limits: Most of the time, I recommend that you set a time during which you need to accomplish a particular goal. It might be within a certain number of days, weeks, or, perhaps, months. The reason is because setting deadlines provides structure, which many people need. Be careful, though. If you fail to accomplish your goal within that defined time frame, you may end up reinforcing your belief that you are a failure. Set the goal, but impose a time limit only if it is needed to help you maintain focus. Sometimes, it doesn't really matter when you complete the task. Whether your goal is to lose weight or to create a piece of art, you are still a success as long as you are making progress. It may not always work when responding to the demands of your boss; but, if there's no need to impose a time constraint, then why add to your anxiety?

Don't Over-Publicize Your Goal: Some professionals recommend that you tell others about your objectives to provide the additional motivation you might need in order to see the task through to completion. Of course, you want to share your goal with those people who will be affected by it. Furthermore, many people benefit by having a 'buddy' with the same goal. I'm advising against making prominent, public announcements. Why set yourself up for public embarrassment if you fail to accomplish your objective? It's just not necessary. In fact, it may encourage others to badger you, especially if you're trying to lose weight. At the next office party when you reach for that extra piece of cake, you are inviting people to remind you of all the calories you are putting into your mouth. Instead of subjecting yourself to public scrutiny, go about achieving your goal, and wait for others to notice that you've shed a few pounds or that your clothes fit better. That's a much better way of doing it.

Dealing with Psychological Barriers: If you are a person who sets a goal, but you never seem to accomplish it, consider the possibility that the reason is not because you don't have the necessary skills to organize your time. Perhaps, instead, you are running into some hand-me-down beliefs. You may have been criticized as a child and told that you were not capable of doing certain things. Or, that you would never amount to anything because every one of your ancestors was totally incompetent when it came to working with their hands, for example. If a parent or some other authority figure instills negative beliefs such as these at an impressionable age, they easily can become self-fulfilling prophesies. Furthermore, beliefs about oneself don't change overnight. Sometimes, the most important, first step in achieving a particular objective is to change the way you see yourself and to start believing that you do have the ability to achieve your dreams.

Do It for Yourself: Make sure that the goal you set is truly your goal and that what you're doing is not intended simply to please someone else. It might please others, but that should not be the primary motivation.

Be Flexible: When setting about to pursue a dream, be flexible. If you have set life-long goals, then you need to review these at least once a year to see if the goals you felt were important when you were in your 20's are still important to you in your 40's. You may have new responsibilities, health problems, or other considerations that limit what is realistic for you to accomplish. So, on a regular basis, subject your goals to re-assessment in much the same way that you subject your beliefs to re-analysis. Answer these questions:

Are your goals new, or did you formulate them years ago but have yet to achieve them? If the latter, why have you been unable to make more headway?

Do you have too many goals and insufficient time to spend working towards them?

Have you wasted time and effort on objectives that had nothing to do with your lifelong goals?

Are your values mirrored in the steps you take to achieve your objectives?

Reflecting on the answers to these questions will shed considerable light on the changes you might need to make in order to begin making progress. If you don't remove hidden obstacles to achieving your goals, positive steps can be discouragingly slow.

What's Your Optimal Time? You may have a surplus of energy, but you may not have it at the times you need it. Many people make the mistake of tackling the things they have to do on the basis of urgency. They fail to take into account that there are times of the day when they are better able to take on certain types of tasks as opposed to others. As the sun progresses from the Eastern horizon to the West, so are our bodies changing. When we first get up in the morning, we have a large amount of the chemical that mobilizes energy. This chemical is called cortisol; and, as the day goes on, the levels gradually drop, bottoming out at about 3:00 in the morning, a time when most people normally are asleep. It then rises when we get out of bed, providing us with the energy we need to make it through the next day. There are also ultradian rhythms. As opposed to a circadian rhythm, which means *about the day*, ultradian rhythms mean *within the day*. One of the best characterizations is the constant shifting in brain dominance.

You've undoubtedly heard of the left versus right-brain. The left-brain is primarily responsible for language and analytical skills. The right-brain, however, is involved more with artistic pursuits. Creating sculptures, music awareness, and music expression depend more upon neurons based in the right hemisphere. Every 90 to 110 minutes, you switch. For part of the day, the electrical activity on one side of the brain is more pronounced than it is on the other. Have you ever found yourself in the middle of a task, where you are in what psychologists would refer to as 'flow' or, in athletics, 'the zone'? You are doing what you need to do almost effortlessly, and it seems as though you could go on forever. Your performance is flawless. The clay is literally coming to life in your hands as you create the piece of art. But, then you take a short break. You return to the task, and the clay literally crumbles in your hands. Or, the report that you had been writing with very little effort becomes impossible to resume. A contributing factor could very well be that you have switched from the side of the brain that would facilitate accomplishing this task. Writing a report depends upon language. That's a left-brain function, while creating a sculpture would require the right.

What you need to do is select the time of day when you are most likely to be able to complete the task at hand. If it requires a certain amount of energy and physical exertion, then select a time of day when your glucocorticoids will be elevated, for example, the morning. If it's a language-based task, then select a time of day when you are more likely to be in your left-hemisphere as opposed to your right. No, you do not need sophisticated electronic equipment to determine which side of the brain is dominant. You very well may be able to determine this by doing the following nasal exercise.

Take a deep breath through your nose. Now do it again, and pay attention through which nostril you are breathing. Obviously, you are probably breathing through both simultaneously; but, if you pay very careful attention, you'll notice that the air is passing more readily through one side as opposed to the other. What facilitates the passage of air is constriction of blood vessels on that side. The more constricted the blood vessels, the more readily air will pass through the corresponding nostril. Vascular constriction is controlled by the autonomic nervous system. Unlike other components of the nervous system, the autonomic nerve do not cross over. What's happening on one side of your body is happening on the same side of your brain. If the air is passing more readily through your left nostril, that means that the blood vessels are not only maximally constricted in your left nostril, but they are also maximally constricted on the left side of your brain. There's going to be relatively more blood flow in the opposite hemisphere. What is the translation of this information? Quite simply, you are in the side of the brain opposite to the nostril that you are breathing through. Just as your electrical activity shifts from one side of the brain to the other in an ultradian type of fashion, so does the ease with which air passes through your nostrils. After you have established which nostril you are breathing through most readily, try it again in about an hour. Chances are, you will have switched.

I realize that this sounds like a rather unscientific approach, but the phenomenon is real. You cannot dispute data, just their interpretation. A number of studies have documented that the switch from the left side to the right does, indeed, occur. Whether it is due to subtle changes in vasoconstriction is not absolutely clear. Regardless of the mechanism whereby the switch is taking place, the fact that changes in the brain occur has been known since antiquity in India. Hunters recognized that there were certain times during the day when they were less likely to be successful as compared with others. They determined when that time of day was on the basis of which nostril they were breathing through. It's 10:00 AM; and at 11:00 AM, you have to have a very important report on your supervisor's desk. You have just switched over, and you are now breathing through your left nostril, which means, of course, that you are in your right-brain. This is not the best side of the brain to be in if you want to achieve flow if your goal is finishing a report. You need to be in your left-brain, which is where language is based; and that, in turn, means that you should be breathing more readily through your right nostril. Some people claim to be able to shift their dominance by forcing themselves to breathe through a particular nostril. By holding your nostril and forcing yourself to breathe through one or the other, it is possible to shift the dominance profile. There are even a few scientific papers documenting that this can be achieved under laboratory conditions, as well. Whether it will work for you is something that you will have to find out.

Sex Rhythms

Much has been written about the tidal-like movement of estrogen and progesterone, which gives rise to physiological and, sometimes, mood changes in pre-menopausal women. But men experience changes associated with fluctuations in testosterone. They can influence performance and feelings on a daily, monthly, annual, and lifetime basis. Coaches and athletes are certainly aware of this. Even in the absence of any identifiable factor, there are times when athletes drop into a performance slump. Most likely, it is due to changes in the anabolic steroid, testosterone. This classic male hormone not only drops the voice an octave or two, but it also can be converted into estrogen. Thus, men also may be subject to mood changes.

Testosterone can fluctuate during the day. It's normally highest in the morning and then drops at around bedtime. Superimposed upon this diurnal rhythm are mini-cycles that take place over a period of 15 to 20 minutes—approximately the interval that some men claim to fantasize about sex. Levels are also more likely to be higher during the fall and prior to the age of 40. Afterwards, there's an approximately 10 percent decline with each, subsequent decade. Of course, levels of stress, exercise, and diet may impact the rate of change. For some men, these variations may be so subtle as to be inconsequential. For others, they may explain noticeable changes in both mental and physical abilities. How can you find out? Try this:

Keep a detailed diary. Record everything that happens pertinent to what you want to accomplish. Do you want to find out why you zone out every day between 3:00 PM and 4:00 PM? Or how you can anticipate in advance those moments when everything you do works out just the way you wanted? Are you in a certain state because of conditioning? Are hormones running the show? You need to track everything, especially diet and time of day. Any rhythmicity would suggest a biological factor. If something happens seemingly at random or correlated only with certain events, chances are it's an environmentally-induced phenomenon. Eventually, you will study each page to determine if there are any consistent correlations. Then, using these data, pick the optimal time to do those things you need to accomplish.

Emotions

As I noted in a previous section, the word emotion is derived from the same root word that gave rise to the word, motivate. And that's exactly what emotions do; they motivate us to take action. While actions come in many forms, from the standpoint of the brain, there are only two. We approach those things associated with positive emotions that often accompany pleasurable events, and avoid those linked with negative emotions that more often are associated with unpleasant things. At one time, it was thought there were only two emotions, those that give rise to pleasure and those that give rise to pain. This turned out to be overly simplistic denying the richness each emotion can bring to our experiences. However, from the standpoint of our fundamental behavior, it is correct. Furthermore, the two emotions cancel each other out.

When giving a lecture on this topic, I'll sometimes ask for a volunteer to demonstrate this principle. Their task seems at first to be fairly straightforward. They have to make themselves cry, and if successful they are told they will receive a one thousand dollar gift card. Often, a third or more of the audience will raise their hands. Indeed, some will race out of their chairs to be the first in line to compete for the prize. That's when I tell them to wait until they gather more information about the task at hand. I explain the rules as follows:

1. They cannot sit in the protective setting of their chair. Instead, they must come to the front of the

room and stand before the entire audience while carrying out the task.

2. They have to be tears of sadness, which means they can't tug at a nose hair or pinch themselves. At this point the number of volunteers has dwindled to less than 10 percent. There's more.

3. They have just one minute to induce the tears, and while attempting to do so, they must arrange their facial muscles into the configuration of a smile. It is rare for anyone to show willingness to continue after hearing these conditions. But just in case there is, I add one more; if they are not successful, they have to give me $1000!

It's quite likely that many people could meet with success if allowed to focus without any distractions upon a painful past experience associated with a great deal of sadness. However, when I begin to add the type of pressure that exists in the real world, it becomes more challenging to experience the desired emotion. They change their minds when they realize there are time constraints and they stand to lose money if unsuccessful. So what does smiling do? It counteracts sadness. Soon after birth, when a baby smiles back at it's mother, that configuration of the facial muscles becomes associated with warmth, security and happiness. In the same way a car muffler will deaden the engine noise by using a baffle to cause echoes of sound waves to reduce the noise, a positive emotion will in this case reduce a negative one. While this exercise serves the intended purpose of illustrating how one can experience Emotional Interference, the example I give is rarely the way things happen in the real world. When facing a deadline or dealing with an unpredictable client, it's invariably fear of failure that blunts the experience of pleasure.

To further drive this point home, I will instruct members of the audience to place their left palm in front of the person to their left, then place their right thumb into the open palm of the person to their right. I then think of a word, which when I shout it out signals that they are to grab the thumb of the person sitting to their right, but to avoid having their thumb trapped in the hand of the person to their left. It sounds simple, but it's not. You see, the brain is required to simultaneously engage two opposite responses; approach (which is grabbing the other person's thumb) and withdrawal (which is keeping yours from being trapped). It seems easy until they try it. The emotions cancel each other and complete success is rare.

There's one more thing you need to understand. Fear wins. In the childhood game of *Rock, Paper, Scissors*, 'fear' is the equivalent of paper to rock, rock to scissors and scissors to paper. Fear has to prevail because ignoring a potential threat could have catastrophic consequences. The brain figures it's better to waste some biological energy and experience a little anxiety even if the threat is not real, then it is to ignore something that might be life threatening. It doesn't matter where the fear originates. It could be directly related to the task at hand, for example the beliefs I listed earlier. Or it could be fear associated with something going on in your personal life. It doesn't matter. Regardless of the source, it spills over and puts you into withdrawal. This may be manifested in a number of ways. A professional tennis player contemplating the fear of losing a match, may delay a millisecond or two before returning a high speed serve. A salesperson may wait before calling the client to finalize a contract. The prospect of losing the sale may prompt a salesperson to delay calling the client in order to spend a little more time rehearsing the pitch. Instead of being motivated to win, they are striving to avoid losing. As a result, the competition closed the deal while they were still mentally rehearsing the possible outcomes. I'm not suggesting you go blindly into a negotiation without preparation. But collect the information you need to win, not to avoid losing. One will result in a belief driven image likely lead to success. The other will shape an image likely to lead to failure. That's because as a result on dwelling upon the things that might go wrong, fear of failure rules the day. Remember, fear triggers withdrawal, including withdrawal from those things you need to do to achieve a goal.

Fear is the emotion of the future. You can be afraid only of those things that have not happened. If it's already happened, you can be angry, disgusted, or sad, but not afraid. What fuels fear is the inability to predict. But after a sufficient amount of time has passed, the fear dissipates when you realize it was unfounded. That does not apply to regret. It's rare that a person is able to recreate the exact circumstances that once existed and have a second chance to experience a missed opportunity. My recommendation is combine the two. Instead of fearing failure, fear the regret you may experience if you don't capitalize on the opportunity before you. Remember, fear is the dominant emotion that overshadows most of the others. You now have a way to convert it into a recipe for success. As I explained previously, subject the beliefs giving rise to fear of failure to constant scrutiny. Ask yourself, *is it justified, is it serving a useful purpose,* and *does if feel right.* Less important than the answers is to engage in this type of process to assess the beliefs that are shaping your images. Remember, it's the image events give rise to, not the event itself, that activates the emotions, which ultimately shape your thoughts and decisions.

How Can You Optimize Success?: Act Like a Winner

For several years I engaged in research designed to find out if a person can use acting skills as a means by which to change their personality. The study came about as a result of an observation I had made many years earlier when studying a person who had been diagnosed with multiple personality disorder. This rare condition is characterized by the display of highly contrasting personalities with sometimes as many as several dozen distinct personalities, each residing in the same body. An experiment was designed whereby several distinct personalities appeared during a limited period of time Before and after each personality appeared, a small amount of blood was taken in order to measure the immune system.

Profound changes in the number of cells as well as their ability to function were observed after certain of the personalities had been in the body. Even though no conclusions can be drawn from any study with just one person, we were, nonetheless, intrigued by the fact that such profound changes in as basic a measure as the number of white cells could be correlated with nothing more than a change in the person's personality. This observation prompted us to design a study to see if a person without any pathology could 'act' a particular emotion and actually elicit changes in their physiology.

Two professional actors played two contrasting roles. You was a very negative, depressive piece, while the other was quite uplifting. The depressive piece was a play called "It's Cold Wanderer, It's Cold." The setting was turn of the century Russia during the mayhem associated with the revolution. The male actor played the role of an assassin who was being interviewed on the eve of his execution by the widow of the politician he had murdered. The play lasted approximately 30 minutes. Then, after a brief intermission, the assassin played the role of Ricky and the widow played the role of Lucy in a stage adaptation of the "I Love Lucy" television series. These plays were presented before different live audiences over a two week period and blood samples were taken before and after each performance. Several changes were observed in immune system measures that were consistent with observations that have been reported in the medical literature indicating that depression may be correlated with impaired immunity. In short, what we found was evidence that by simply acting in a depressed way, certain measures of the immune system actually are decreased. Bill Moyers, when he produced the Emmy Award winning program, Healing and the Mind for PBS, felt that this study was such a convincing demonstration of how the mind influences the immune system, he used it to open the entire series.

Competitive sport is a different type of laboratory but nonetheless one that has yielded meaningful results. Results that are reflected not just in numbers that can be analyzed statistically, but in a real life laboratory in the form of gold medals and world championships. The same process used by the record setting speed skater, Dan Jansen, can be used by virtually anyone. It's a technique inspired by my acting study and developed by the performance coach, Dr. Jim Loehr. He instructed his clients to literally act like winners. Here's how you might apply this technique.

Think back to when you were on top of the world. Everything was going perfectly. It might have been in high school when your sports team won the regional championship or you accomplished a goal, which you had thought was absolutely beyond your reach. Try to recall as many details about that event as you can. The way you carried yourself, the expression on your face, and in your mind. Recreate that moment. If a particular piece of music reminds you of that moment or if you have a photograph that will help trigger the feeling state, use it. And then practice achieving that same state on demand. Athletes don't win championships because they inherited the skills. Skills are acquired and only after years of ritualistic practice. That is exactly what you need to do as well. Practice achieving the Ideal Performance State so that when confronted with the task of performing when you don't really feel like it, you can put yourself almost instantly into the appropriate state of mind and body. The arena that you work in is not that different from the arena athletes work in. At least from the standpoint of stress. Just as preoccupation with a thought or a particular attitude can interfere with the coordinated movements needed to win a race, so can similar preoccupation interfere with your ability to achieve a goal.

Creating mental images works as well. Scientists have long known that if you are placed in front of an object the electrical profile in the area of your brain that mediates visual information will show a distinct pattern of activity as you stare at the object. Then, if you are asked to close your eyes and imagine that object, a very similar electrical profile is revealed. Think of the higher brain centers as being the equivalent of a television monitor. The emotional computer in the brain is sitting in front of it watching. You know that if you're watching a film on television it doesn't matter whether that film has been pre-recorded or whether it's coming in live through the cable system. Your response to the images on that television screen will be identical, regardless of the source. In fact if it's a very suspenseful film you may experience fear and anxiety as you sit there fully aware that you are in no danger whatsoever. But the images that arrive in the brain elicit the same response as though you really were somehow in the scene that is being depicted on the film.

The key to achieving goals is quite simply to substitute appropriate images to create the optimal performance state. I'm not suggesting that you go so far as to just create wonderful positive images. That if you think that everything is rosy it will become that way, that if you express love and joy that everything will fall into place. That's not a very pragmatic solution if you are faced with difficult circumstances that are keeping you from accomplishing your goal. But what you can and should do is to view what is happening not as an obstacle but rather as a challenge. Reflect upon how emotions such as anger and fear impact your brain and ultimately your physiology. These processes may have served you very well back in the Stone Age when it was necessary to protect your territory or elude a saber tooth tiger. But those same primitive reflexes and instincts can be devastating in today's modern society. Use imaging and acting as processes to channel negative emotions into a positive force that will enable you to achieve not only the Optimal Performance State but also an optimal state of health. You don't need to attend acting school to master this technique. Here are six steps to achieve the winning state.

1. Keep your arms and hands relaxed and let your hands hang about four inches from your hips.
2. Hold your shoulders back.
3. Keep your chin level with the ground and do not let your head drop.
4. Walk with a strong stride on the balls of your feet.

5. Keep your eyes focused on the person you are dealing with or the ball if it's a tennis match, and during times of the break, continue to keep them focused on some appropriate object. If it's a presentation, it might be your notes. Avoid allowing your eyes to wander because this communicates to those around you that your mind is wandering.

6. Keep up this posture even when you're taking a break. Even a brief lapse is sufficient to cause you to sometimes lose control.

And remember to customize this formula. If you can, obtain video tapes or photographs of when you were at your peak. Stop the video and study exactly what you looked like when you were in that peak form. Try to reproduce it under all circumstances when you want to be in your peak. Conversely, avoid that look associated with losing or when things were not going well. In short, act like a winner and you will become a winner. That's as true of life as it is of sports.

For many real world performers, the pressure dynamics, the consequences of failure, and the levels of energy expenditure exceed anything ever studied in competitive sport. In a real sense, you may be the athlete of all athletes. And regardless of your occupation, there are times when you have to be able to perform even though you may not feel like it. It's a sad commentary but true that no one really cares. If you are being paid to do a job, you are expected to complete the task regardless of what might be going on in your personal life. If there is a deadline and your employer is paying you a generous salary to accomplish a goal, then by golly, you have to perform. When your favorite football team takes to the field you don't care if the star athlete has a sprained ankle. Because of the salaries that professional athletes can command, you expect that person to go out and play as though there were nothing wrong. You expect them to wrap up that ankle and perform flawlessly. Many of us are also expected to perform even though we may not want to. The ones who can are the people who are successful in life and also very healthy. They can achieve the Optimal Performance State on demand.

So how do athletes prepare themselves for the brutality of their playing fields? How do they protect their health and happiness in the face of such extraordinary demands placed on their minds and bodies? Simply put, they train for it. They train everyday—mentally, physically and emotionally to withstand the forces. And since the competition and stress in your life often exceeds those of athletes, you've got to go into training every day to become stronger, more resilient and more flexible mentally, physically and emotionally. In competitive sport, it's known that without balance, sustained success is impossible. Body, mind, health, happiness, spirit, performance, and emotions are all part of a mosaic. The more we slice them up, separate them, make them discrete categories in themselves, the more mistakes we make and the more we miss the truth. Everything is connected to everything else. The Optimal Performance

State is related to the Optimal Immunologic State which is related to the Optimal State of Personal Happiness. Real answers are interdisciplinary. They are not quick fixes. They are systematic solutions that fully embrace the inseparable links between the mind, body and spirit. This understanding rests at the very core of this program.

Stress

Although much of the discussion thus far has dealt with the field of athletics, you too are an athlete. It is unlikely that you will ever by called upon to perform before tens of thousands of people in a sports arena. But we all have to perform in a type of performance setting. In the home when resolving a family conflict. Or in the classroom, the emergency room, or perhaps the office you happen to work in. You have to drive energy, concentration, and focus to accomplish important goals. In fact, for many of us the mental, physical, and emotional demands associated with our playing fields exceed anything that transpires in competitive sports. Many non-sport performance arenas require 10-12 hours of daily, focused energy expenditure. Talk about ultra marathons! And how about pressure? Mistakes in sport can cost you the game but in real life, mistakes can be far more devastating. Airline pilots, surgeons, law enforcement officers, medical personnel of all kinds, air traffic controllers, nuclear power plant operators, school bus drivers, firemen, power line workers, and on and on. The way that you handle stress may also impact your family's physical health. A study at the University of California has revealed that stress is a major problem for children. As a result of measuring heart rate and blood pressure, it was found that about 20 percent of the children were very tense. These were preschool age children. These were also the children who, when they attended a day care center, were found to be more susceptible to infections and to have decreased immunity. The big factor turned out to be their home life. Any major crisis outside of school, including moving, death of a parent, or divorce, rendered the stressed out children to be particularly prone to lung infections. A stable home environment, however, resulted in extremely low rates of illness. The same happens in adults. A person is far more likely to develop a cold or flu during times of emotional upheaval. That's because the chemistry of the fight of flight response takes a toll on the white cells our immune system depends upon. Decreased attention, lethargy, as well as lapses in memory and judgment are additional symptoms of stress. These are just some of the reasons you need to start thinking about how best to cope with stress in your life. Especially since the situation is getting worse.

People are spending more and more time at work surrounded by stress and with less time to engage in pleasure. The so-called 'disposable time' for the average male worker dropped from 40 to 36 hours per week from 1935 to 1965. By 1973 it had further dropped to just 26 hours per week, and by 1990, male workers were getting an average of 17 hours of free time per week. Now, well into the 21st century, the number continues to decline. It's now less than half the amount of time our grandfather's had to enjoy the pleasures of life. The outlook is not much brighter for women. Why is this so? It all started as we attempted to support a higher standard of living. We had to work longer and harder in order to pay for that essential second car, the large TV, or other electronic gadgets that have become icons of society. What little time you do have is not spent in healthy pursuits. As a consequence of these expensive habits, we are now in debt to credit card companies and mortgage companies to the tune of trillions of dollars per year. Essentially, we started working harder to pay off our debts. Now there's an even more compelling reason to work hard. To avoid losing our jobs. Stocks have soared but not without a human toll. While the stockholders of major corporations were rejoicing, hundreds of thousands of employees were terminated as companies downsized. That downsizing is occurring in companies where a person thought that their job was good for life. Such downsizing breeds increased competition at every single level. The common assumption is that if you don't work longer hours than your co-worker, then you are the one most likely to be tapped next time some trimming has to be done. In addition, those people who remain on the job have to assume the responsibilities of those who have now left. There's also very little satisfaction associated with jobs that people hold today. Many people stand all day on an assembly line doing the same repetitive task. Or you may be lost in a sea of desks without any indication of what fruits your labor has born. There's very little job satisfaction, which leads to a number of common illnesses, ranging from coronary arterial disease to infection. Ultimately, this impacts upon the company because job dissatisfaction in the number one variable that predicts whether or not a workman's compensation claim is likely to be filed. No wonder many of us are feeling cynical, anxious, depressed, and tired and why many millenials have no expectation of remaining at one job for their entire professional life.

Dealing with Adversity and Set Backs

A Quick Fix

I've explained ways for dealing with the understanding and eventual changing of your beliefs. But those techniques won't do you much good during an emergency. When you find yourself in the midst of an emotional crisis, that is not the time to be sitting back and saying, *"What are my beliefs? And is it my belief or somebody else's? What were those seven questions?"* The process I have described is fine for making long-term adjustments; however, occasionally, you need to be able to do something immediately. And one of the most effective ways of putting the brakes on the emotional response and maintaining control so that you can remain focused on your goal is to boost your sense of satisfaction. There's only one thing that is consistently characteristic of a happy person. It's not age, gender, wealth, or health. Happiness is experienced when you are truly satisfied with what you currently have. Be careful. Dissatisfaction is an excellent motivator. You should not be satisfied with things that are within your power to improve. But when you have done your best and are satisfied with your circumstances, then happiness will be the result. Here's a very simple way to improve your level of satisfaction. Complete this statement three times in the context of whatever is happening:

I am glad I am not _____.

If you find yourself caught in gridlock with no way of making it to the important meeting, complete this statement by saying, *"I am glad I am not a part of the accident that is causing this traffic jam."* Or if your child comes home from school with failing grades, complete this statement by saying, *"I am glad I did not just receive a call from the emergency room regarding my child."* It's called reframing, and it may explain why people who have dealt with a great deal of adversity are often better able to deal with future crises. As a result of having successfully endured and survived a bad situation, they learn that everything is temporary. In the words of the Anglo-Saxon poem *Deor*, "This, too, shall pass." Now, when they find themselves in a quandary, they can reflect upon the previous incident, which will make the current episode seem trivial by comparison.

I was living in Grenada during the Marxist revolution in 1979 and recall dozens of panic-stricken American medical students seeking any avenue off the island. They even offered local fishermen vast sums to transport them to safety in small, dilapidated boats. Thank goodness the fishermen had the wisdom to decline. There's no way that many of those boats would have safely made the crossing to the next island. On the other hand, the expatriates who resided on the island took it all in stride. One resident had lived through several similar revolutions in Africa. Others had lived in London during World War II and had endured the relentless nightly bombings during the Blitz. Their perspective was very different. They had been through far worse and had survived. Therefore, they were confident that they could do so this time. By reflecting upon a previous experience or by simply imagining something worse, you find yourself becoming more satisfied with your present circumstances. What many people do is just the opposite. They make things worse by completing the statement:

I wish I were _____.

That sequence of words is a recipe for dissatisfaction. *I wish I had a better car, a bigger house, or a more meaningful job* will simply reinforce your perception that you are dissatisfied.

Optimism
The Russians were preparing to launch the first satellite into space; American advisors were venturing into

Vietnam; and Ruth Fisher was my sixth-grade teacher. Yet, with a stroke of her pen, she had as great an impact on shaping my life as those world events would have on shaping the following decades. *"Nicholas doesn't pay attention. He wastes time, and he fails to follow instructions,"* she wrote on the back of my C- and D-strewn report card. Hardly words of praise, yet they instilled in me a sense of confidence and optimism. The lasting message was conveyed between the words: *"Nicholas doesn't . . . wastes time . . . fails to follow instructions."* It was *I* who was in command. My lackluster grades were not the consequence of a low IQ or some genetically-inspired inability to learn. Instead, those D's were the result of my actions—or, rather, lack of actions. At any time, I *chose*; I could have earned A's and B's. All I had to do was start paying attention and start following instructions. That was my choice, and it required no help from anyone.

Pity the poor student who, despite paying attention and following instructions, still failed. Chances are, the teacher would have concluded, *John is just not good at math* or *Mary just doesn't do well on tests.* John and Mary will learn that they have a problem with no clear solution in hand. They are being told that there is a problem with *them.* I was told there was a problem with my *choices.* As a consequence, I came to recognize that most of life's hurdles are temporary setbacks and are capable of being overcome. I learned to be optimistic. Here are some other things I've learned along the way:

- Nothing in life is permanent. While lessons learned early in life can have a lasting impact, pessimism can be changed. The steps are the foundation of cognitive psychotherapy.

- Learn to succeed through failure in the same way many successful CEOs have. Despite being labeled as dyslexic or ADD as children, they found that the problem was not their style but the mismatch with their environment. Optimism is realistic, not positive-thinking. It is recognizing that doing something can make a difference. It is no wonder that optimism predicts a reduced incidence of cancer and improved immunity. Optimists also have more friends since they are more fun to be around. Social support is yet another pathway to optimal health.

Clearly, optimism is a trait engrained during early childhood. However, that's water under the bridge. You can't go back and rewrite history. So what are your current options? What steps can you take to instill a sense of optimism long after having a pessimistic explanatory style imposed upon your psyche? There are things you can do, but it won't be easy. That's because it may require reprogramming your brain. In the face of adversity, you are likely to respond to a threat by engaging in either approach or avoidance behaviors. In the extreme, you would either fight or run away. Associated with the approach system is optimism. It's highly unlikely that you would engage in a behavior unless you anticipated a positive outcome. Enthusiasm and pride would generally occur when moving toward a goal. In contrast, another system is associated with withdrawal from an aversive environment. Negative affect, perhaps in the form of disgust or fear, will generally be associated with putting distance between yourself and the source of the threat. Your tendency to withdraw will keep you from your goal.

Martin Seligman has conducted a number of studies revealing that people's individual coping styles will have an impact on their response to threat. People who recognize that adversity does not have to permeate every aspect of their life, that adversity is temporary, and, largely, the result of external events, have an optimistic explanatory style and, generally, will rebound faster from stress-inducing events. They will view the event as a challenge and engage in approach behaviors. Their attitude is, *"I can do this."* In contrast, those who personalize events and embrace the belief that every aspect of their life will be negatively and permanently impacted are said to have a pessimistic explanatory style. They tend to view adversity as an obstacle and engage in avoidance behaviors which will keep them from achieving goals.

Anatomy of Optimism

A specific part of the brain called the prefrontal cortex appears to be partially responsible for determining whether a person will approach or avoid. This bi-lobed structure is located above the orbits at the front of the brain. Different regions of this structure are responsible for shaping your responsiveness to events. The left side contributes to positive feelings since patients with damage to this region are more likely to be depressed. This observation is consistent with electrophysiological data. When healthy people are exposed to emotion-eliciting events, there is increased activity on the left side of the brain during times when the person is experiencing happiness, and there is more activity on the right side of the brain when they are sad.

So often, we tend to think that if something is associated with an event in the brain, it must be the cause of a behavior and not itself subject to behavioral influences. That is not true of the prefrontal lobes. A technique called mindfulness has been shown capable of bringing about not only a change in brain activity but also a change in outlook. It's a technique that requires instruction and practice. Therefore, it is beyond the scope of this audio book to provide an in-depth description of the protocol. Nonetheless, it involves the induction of a meditative state, while maintaining an awareness of something in the environment. Usually, it is an aroma, a sound, or some other feature, which, otherwise, would not be a part of your conscious awareness. When taking steps to change your outlook, do not replace pessimism with positive thinking. That is not a feature of optimism. Bad things happen, and, when they do, there may be nothing to justify a rosy outlook. As defined by Seligman, optimism pertains to how you perceive adversity. It's more about non-negative thinking than it is about being positive. Seligman has formulated what he refers to as the ABC technique for replacing a pessimistic explanatory style with one that is optimistic.

- **Adversity:** Identify the problem minus any feelings. It's merely a description of what has happened.
- **Beliefs:** Examine the beliefs that are shaping your response.
- **Consequences:** Reflect upon your actions as well as their consequences.

This is really a modification of cognitive therapy, used extensively by mental health workers. The basic formula, which you will engage in yourself, is as follows:

- Identify the automatic thoughts, which make you feel worse.
- Consider opposite interpretations as you dispute these harmful thoughts.
- Create different explanations.
- Develop a strategy to distract yourself from negative thoughts.
- Examine carefully the depression-inducing beliefs that give rise to your pessimism.

Conditioned Habits

Earl Chace was the curator at the Black Hills Reptile Gardens where during most of the 1960's, I wrestled alligators and milked rattlesnakes to earn money for college. I was 14 when I set out on a Greyhound bus from my home in Massachusetts to the

Black Hills of South Dakota. Chace, what we called him because the owners name was also Earl, was a kind and caring man who was amongst a handful of people who kept a watchful eye on me during those carefree summers. His early years had been spent as curator of insects at the Bronx Zoo in New York. He was also a talented pianist and organ player, a skill that provided extra money when he created the musical backdrop for silent movies that dominated the theaters during the 1930's. It was difficult to move about his cramped living room, for most of the floor space was covered with a large piano and organ. He continued to play for pleasure throughout the years I worked with him. It was with a great deal of sadness when decades later, I paid him a visit only to learn that Alzheimers Disease had robbed him of his memory. Indeed, I quickly realized when I visited that he had no idea who I was. But while he was unable to recall any of his past experiences, when led to the piano, music flowed from fingers as they darted across the keys.

That type of memory is called implicit memory and occurs in other ways as well. Indeed, it is the foundation of many things we do without thought. These automatic memories were most notably characterized during the last century by the Russian physiologist, Ivan Pavlov. During the course of studying the digestive system of dogs, he observed that after pairing certain sounds with food, the sound by itself became capable of eliciting salivation and the release of stomach secretions. Metronomes, tuning forks, and a bell were just of few of many forms of stimuli, which, after a sufficient number of repetitions, became capable of eliciting the release of digestive secretions in the absence of meat. All that was needed was a brief association of the sound with the meat, which through the olfactory and visual senses was able to naturally activate gastric pathways. It was called Classical or Pavlovian conditioning, a discovery that earned him the Nobel Prize. At the subconscious level, the dogs had learned to respond in a highly specific way to an otherwise inert sound after it had been paired with the natural stimulus. Obstacles to achieving goals can become automatic responses to similar, unintended conditioned cues.

My job at the Reptile Gardens was extracting venom from rattlesnakes and wrestling alligators during the course of shows designed to entertain visiting tourists. There were other less dangerous shows, including a gallery featuring trained farm animals. The façade was of an old western town. The show began with a cow, who when she rang a bell by pulling a rope, signaled a half dozen young chickens to run down the make belief street to the school. Next was a rabbit, posing as a banker, that had been trained to count bank notes. He was followed by a dancing chicken, then a goat that rammed his way out of a jail cell, followed by the final act, Grubstake Charlie who deposited a large gold nugget into a container that he pushed on rails. Grubstake was a pig. What was remarkable about the show is once the announcer opened the window so the cow could ring the bell, the rest of the show ran on autopilot. The ringing bell was the Pavlovian-like stimulus that prompted the chickens to run down the street, which signaled the rabbit to count the money. When he was done, the music came on, signaling the chicken to scratch at the surface, which appeared to the audience to be a dance accompanied by the music. Each animal responded to a cue provided by the previous one. It was a cleverly thought out sequence whereby once started, continued through to the end. Each show proceeded like clockwork with little for the emcee to do except activate the food dispenser so once finished, each animal received a reward.

Without realizing it, many of us run the routine parts of our lives this way. Without thinking about it the morning alarm rouses a person from bed. That prompts a trip to the bathroom where the person might shower, then brush their teeth before dressing and putting on their shoes. Chances are, each part of the routine is done exactly the same way each day. Each day the toothpaste is spread in a consistent way, the teeth are brushed starting on the same side of the mouth, and then the clothes are put on in the exact same sequence as are the shoes. Those types of conditioned responses define our days at work and at play. Each step signals the next with barely any conscious awareness of the exact details of how or why the task is being carried out. From the time a person awakens , he is subconsciously responding to environmental triggers that elicit a variety of responses, some with beneficial consequences and some that are detrimental. This type of automatic learning, if carefully nurtured, can propel you to success, or if overlooked, can dash your hopes and dreams. Earlier, I spoke about the impact belief driven emotions can have upon the attainment of goals. What if certain beliefs or emotions become associated with a particular time of day, or in a specific location you are at on a daily basis. You may find yourself losing the motivation to continue because certain thoughts are being triggered by the time of day, a fragrance or some other subconscious cue. How do you find out of this is happening? Keep a detailed diary of when motivation-reducing thoughts occur. Write down everything associated with that state. Time of day, weather conditions, song playing on the radio, or anything else that may consistently become associated with those self-destructive thoughts.

Building a Reserve of Motivation

You need motivation if you are to achieve any goal, and it is something you have to learn, and then practice. In addition, you have only a certain amount and when you use it up dealing with hassles, it depletes your reserve for additional setbacks. Therefore, the more you start with, the greater your likelihood for success despite stressful setbacks.

Experiments with student volunteers have revealed that when asked to resist a highly desirable object, it predictably requires more will power to do so than when asked to resist a less desirable one. That's certainly not an unexpected finding. The greater the desire for something, the harder it is to resist. The next task was to solve a puzzle that, unbeknownst to the students, was impossible to complete. The objective was to determine if using up a larger amount of will power during the first challenge, would prompt them to give up sooner on the subsequent problem solving task compared with volunteers who used a lesser amount of motivation. It did. The students who had expended negligible amount of will power ignoring the undesirable object had greater motivation to persevere with the second task. They spent a large amount of time experimenting with different approaches, and even seemed to enjoy the challenge. Not so the students who had to resist the desirable object and therefore expended a lot more of their motivation-reserve. When confronted with the unsolvable puzzle they quickly began to express their frustrations, and it wasn't long before they gave up.

That's what happened to me during the Ultimate Florida Challenge I mentioned at the start of this program. You'll recall that on the first day of the race, I broke a critical part on the boat that set me back nearly 15 hours, while I rounded up the parts I would need to undertake the necessary repairs. On another day, I hit an oyster bar late at night and damaged the pedal drive on my Hobie sit on top kayak. Trying to make up lost time, I pushed too hard in very strong winds up the Atlantic coast and snapped the mast. Sleep deprivation resulted in my showing poor judgment causing the capsize of my boat in the ocean off Jacksonville. I eventually caught up with the closest competitor, however, it was early morning and while he was breaking camp after a restful night, I was arriving exhausted at the start of the portage. After loading the heavy boat onto the cart, I set out only to experience my first flat tire. Then the second. By the time I experienced my third flat, I had run out of motivation to continue. Over the 800 miles of the preceding weeks, every ounce of motivation had been drained and I dropped out.

Perhaps the most common reason people fail to follow through and achieve success is because, like me, they deplete their motivation-reserve. At my corporate headquarters at Saddlebrook Resort near Tampa, Florida, I design team-building events for corporate clients who are seeking to improve their productivity, leadership skills, health or any number of other outcomes. Each program is customized to meet the company's goals. I will have two teams solve one of two different tasks. One is very challenging since it requires them to remove an object inside a roped off area without touching the object with their hands. Instead, they have to use ropes and bungee cords. In addition, the team members are blindfolded; all except the leader who can see, but only give oral instructions to those who can't. The leader is not allowed to touch any of the resources. The object they have to move is a container filled with water. Every time water spills, they have to start over. Needless to say, this can be a very frustrating activity, although after about 50 minutes, most teams eventually meet with success. Next, they proceed to another task, which requires them to assemble 14 boards to match a printed diagram. It, too, requires about the same amount of time since each board must be aligned in exactly the right way for the notches to align. However, it is less frustrating that the task requiring them to move the object while blindfolded. If the objective of the team-building event is to understand the obstacles to success, I'll have them complete the board assembly task either after a fun, low frustration activity, or the high frustration one involving blindfolds. Over the past 15 years, and working with hundreds of major corporations, I have found that, when the board assembling task follows the activity with blindfolds, will result in more grumbling about how difficult it is, and along with an additional 20 minutes to eventually complete it. What has happened is during the completion of the initial frustrating task they have depleted their motivation-reserve resulting in reduced desire to continue and often the need for more time to achieve success. Sometimes, the second task can be finished only after I step in and provide hints regarding the solution. In summary, it's easier to lose your motivation when something else has depleted it.

Think of motivation as being comparable to a muscle. With repeated use, fatigue sets in and your ability to hold a heavy weight declines. But with practice, you can increase both strength and endurance. Training results in an increase in the ability to store energy, as well as the capacity to use oxygen. The same phenomena applies to building your motivation. When you practice following a routine, especially one you have to summons more than an average amount of will power to complete, your ability to follow through gradually increases. You can see for yourself. Set a goal to exercise at the same time each morning. It can be in whatever form you want, and for an amount of time you can devote to the workout each day.

On some days, you'll look forward to the routine, while on others, you may have to force yourself to just start. Once you establish a routine of completing the exercise regimen, you'll gradually find it becomes easier to keep it up, in part because the exercise becomes conditioned to the time of day and preceding activities. Furthermore, you'll discover it becomes easier to follow through with other, unrelated tasks. You will still find it more difficult to remain motivated after a succession of frustrating challenges, but when you start out with a greater reserve of motivation, you'll find you can still achieve success. Think of it as bulking up your motivation neurons. Sadly, there are many people who face an excessive amount of frustration, which causes them to lose the motivation to do much of anything except the easiest and most mundane tasks. In the extreme, it's manifested as depression.

Frustrations are not the only impediment to seeing things through. Just performing tasks can be as well, especially if they continue for an extended period of time. Research has shown that the amount of time expended to finish a task is followed by a period of inertia. The more time to complete the task, the longer the period of inactivity is likely to be. In experimental psychology, this is called the plateau. For many years, I've taught medical and nursing students. After a major exam, several days will pass before the level of classroom engagement is restored to the pre-exam level. Students attend class, but fewer hands are raised when I ask questions, and if I call on someone at random, they are not as likely to know the answer because they lacked the motivation to read in advance the assignment. Isaac Newton's observations during the course of research delving into thermodynamics applies not only to physics, but human behavior as well; for every action, there is an equal and opposite reaction. Problems arise when people try to override these natural rhythms of stress and recovery in their quest for greater productivity. After a period of stress, they fail to balance it with a comparable amount of equal and opposite recovery.

There's no easy solution. Indeed, it may be best to simply allow time to restore order to the brain's motivation-systems. After all, muscles must have a period of rest after a strenuous workout, just as people need an interval of sleep following each day of activity. It follows then that a person will have the least number of impediments to accomplishing goals if they pursue them after a period of rest. That's why I recommend that my clients schedule the most challenging tasks during the morning hours after a night of restful sleep. Tackling them in close proximity to another challenging task will more likely result in failure for the same reason a marathoner is not likely to perform optimally if the competition follows a day of physical exertion. Remember, your Motivation-Reserve has many parallels to muscle tissue including the need to recover.

Because I Don't Have the Energy

Unless you have sufficient energy, you'll lack both the will and the ability to achieve goals. There is probably no greater barrier to physical and emotional well-being than fatigue. Failure to get a good night's sleep is invariably the problem—and it is a costly one. The sleep debt in the United States makes the economic debt look trivial by comparison. Over 40 million Americans suffer from sleep disorders. More than 200,000 traffic accidents occur each year because of driver fatigue, and lack of sleep is the cause of 33% of fatal truck accidents. Studies at Stanford University have revealed that drowsy drivers are actually more impaired than most drunken drivers. All totaled, the direct and indirect costs resulting from sleep disorders and fatigue may be as much as $116 billion a year. It's time to start viewing chronic, insufficient rest as a physical disability. It's imperative that you take steps to deal with it. If you don't, you won't be able to achieve the goals you have set, because you lack the energy.

THE TOP CAUSES OF FATIGUE

- Too much work and not enough recreation
- Iron deficiency
- Sleep apnea
- Depression
- Emotional loss
- Thyroid problems
- Recent illness
- Snoring partners
- Sedentary lifestyle

THE SOLUTION

There is also a serious problem in that most people's circadian rhythms run faster than society's clocks. Many internal, biological clocks are on a 26-hour cycle, while the world operates on a 24-hour day. There are things you can do, though, to reset your internal clock. Expose yourself to sunlight as soon as possible after rising. Light signals the brain to set most of the body's biological clocks. If you suspect a medical cause, then guidance from a health care professional is clearly warranted. Otherwise, consider doing some of the following:

Get low impact exercise early in the day. It stimulates your mind plus sets in motion a series of physiological events that result in your body gradually slowing down over the course of the day.

Get out of bed if you haven't fallen asleep within 20 minutes. Lying there worrying about not being able to sleep only protracts the problem. Do something boring—C-SPAN and local government access cable channels are excellent to watch, or read one of those dry trade journals you've brought home from work.

Relax. Use progressive muscle relaxation exercises, deep breathing, or simply count sheep. By concentrating on such efforts, you block troublesome thoughts, which can keep you awake.

Drink a glass of warm milk. Yes, mother was right. We now know why. Milk contains the amino acid, tryptophan, which creates a chemical chain reaction in the brain that helps induce sleep. But, if you suffer from indigestion or acid reflux, milk can actually intensify such gastric discomforts. Experiment to see if this is an option.

Watch what you eat. Fatigue may be due to eating the wrong foods. Studies have shown that approximately two hours after consuming a meal rich in carbohydrates, you will experience fatigue as well as impaired performance on tests requiring speed and concentration. That's because the consumption of carbohydrates facilitates the transport of tryptophan into the brain. The more tryptophan that gets into the brain, the more there is available to be converted into serotonin, a neurotransmitter that stimulates sleep. Timing is everything. Save carbohydrates for dinner, not for the lunch you might consume a couple of hours before having to go into a high-powered, demanding meeting.

Get something hot. There are health benefits associated with ingesting hot peppers and sauces that contain capsaicin, which imparts the hot flavor. But don't have a snack with Tabasco sauce just before you go to bed; it may trigger indigestion. That might be what's waking you up in the middle of the night.

Smoking cigarettes can disrupt your sleep cycle. Carbon monoxide, which is found in tobacco smoke, can interfere with the ability of red blood cells to transport oxygen throughout the body. The less oxygen you have, the less energy you're going to have. Smoking also can impede blood flow and the transport of oxygen by triggering the accumulation of mucous in both the windpipe and the bronchial tubes. This, in turn, will constrict blood vessels and the oxygenation of cells in the body.

Avoid caffeine, especially after about 5:00 in the afternoon, and remember there is as much caffeine in a can of cola as there is in half an average cup of coffee. Perhaps, you were able to get away with drinking huge amounts of this and other caffeine-containing beverages when you were younger. But, as you age and your metabolism slows, it's going to take longer for the body to break the caffeine into its various metabolites. Therefore, the caffeine will remain in your system for a longer period of time. Just because you were able to get away with drinking large amounts of coffee as a student, don't be surprised if those old habits are associated with some consequences later in life.

Stay away from sleeping pills. The benzodiazepines and barbiturates are addictive, and eventually you'll have no choice but to take these medications if you're going to get any sleep at all. Your sleep becomes conditioned to their ingestion. You also should avoid nightcaps. One national survey reports that 29% of people who report difficulty sleeping rely upon alcohol in order to induce a state of relaxation. There's no question that alcohol will induce a state of sleep, but the quality of the sleep you get is lowered, and it's almost guaranteed that you will be prone to waking up, usually about four to five hours after you fall asleep. Alcohol also can impair your ability to take in oxygen. It causes over-relaxation of the muscles and inhibits the respiratory system. The net result is a reduction in your ability to breathe efficiently. All of these things reduce levels of energy.

Create a diversion. There are lots of things you can do to divert yourself, so find a technique that you feel comfortable with and use it. Whatever you do, do it vividly. If you are counting sheep, then visualize each sheep in your mind in order to block intrusive thoughts. Concentrate on your body relaxing, and chances are you won't even recall what number you got to before you fell asleep. You also can count your blessings, adding a sense of joy or gratitude to your relaxation.

There is nothing wrong with healthy worrying. It's only when the worrying interferes with sleep or other functions you have to perform that it's a problem. Set aside time to worry in order to get it out of your system. While you are doing this, think about what it is you're going to do the next day. List the most important tasks you need to accomplish, so that when you awaken, you'll know exactly what needs to be done. And don't do your worrying in bed or in your favorite chair. Otherwise, the bed will trigger worrying, just as Pavlov's bell triggered salivation in his dogs.

Turn the clock. Don't have your clock staring at you next to the bed, so that every time you open your eyes, you are aware of how late it is and the fact that you are still not asleep.

Cool down. What enables you to fall asleep is a subtle drop in body temperature. You can fool your body into activating processes that lower your temperature by jumping into a hot tub or taking a hot bath about an hour before you are ready for bed. The brain will be fooled into thinking you are in danger of dying from hyperthermia. Consequently, it activates processes designed to lower your body temperature sufficiently to compensate for the extra heat. When you leave the source of heat, those processes continue to work, so your body temperature actually drops below normal as the brain temporarily overcompensates. You'll have to experiment to determine exactly how much in advance, you need to do this. Exercise also will work. When you exercise, you temporarily increase your core body temperature. Just make certain that you work out early in the evening so that your body has a chance to cool down and to enter into that over-compensation stage at the time you want to sleep.

Exercise. If you are a man in your 50's, you might be waking in the middle of the night to go to the bathroom. As men age, the prostate gland can swell and partially block the urethra. This triggers the need for frequent urination. Obviously, if you cut back on fluid intake before going to bed, this will help; however, a small amount of light exercise an hour before bedtime will work as well. Don't do anything aerobic, simply some very easy, stretching exercises or a short, five-minute walk. This will stimulate the circulation of fluids through the kidneys, and it will prompt you to get rid of a little more fluid before you go to bed.

Establish a sleep pattern, and make sure that you stay with it. Sleep is one of the easiest things to condition in humans. If you train your body to get used to falling asleep at a certain time of night, it's more likely to happen.

CAUTION

Realize that sleep disorders and fatigue may be secondary to an illness, which cannot be regulated through behavior or supplements. For that reason, it is important to have a thorough physical examination to rule out such a cause.

Even after a restful night's sleep, you still need to maintain your energy during the day. That's best done with the right food. Since food is the fuel of the body, you'd think that with more, you'd be able to go further and last longer. To a certain extent, that is true. The average person needs between about 1500 and 2000 calories per day to keep the body going and to make it through the workday. However, more is less important than type and time when it comes to having energy. Lack of energy is what erodes your motivation to achieve goals and keeps you from doing what you want to do. Ask an athlete about 'hitting the wall' or 'bonking.' These expressions refer to the almost total collapse of the body, usually at a point midway through a long-endurance event. Blood sugar drops, and the athlete's energy level bottoms out. It can happen to anyone, though, and will if you eat too much or too little, at the wrong time of day, or in the wrong proportions of protein, carbohydrate, and fat. The following tips are the ones that many endurance athletes use. If the guidelines work for people who push their physical limits for hours on end, imagine what they could do for you.

Graze. Instead of eating three square meals a day, as prescribed by our culture, eat five or six meals of roughly 200 to 300 calories each. When you eat a larger amount, the extra will trigger a surge of insulin in order to place excess blood glucose into cells. That alone is not a problem. But, it becomes one when you consume large numbers of calories, especially in the form of a high glycemic index food such as white rice. Because these foods are more rapidly converted into blood sugar, the insulin rise is quite abrupt. This, in turn, prompts the pancreas to produce a bit too much insulin, causing more sugar than intended to go into cells. Remember the sluggish feeling you experience after a big meal? Now you know why. Another way to trigger excess insulin and the same drop in blood sugar is to eat a candy bar. While not a guaranteed solution to avoid such insulin surges, a good place to start is by spreading the calories you need over 6 smaller meals instead of the traditional 3. Now your blood sugar will be more constant during the day since you are eliminating the need for an insulin surge and too great a drop in blood sugar. You'll also be less likely to overeat.

Consume Adequate Protein. The more muscle you have, the more calories you burn without doing anything. That's one of the reasons people who are lean and have lots of muscle can get away with eating large portions without gaining excess weight. Building muscle requires adequate protein in your diet. There's considerable information about the amount of protein you should consume relative to carbohydrate, and there's no telling what the latest fad will call for at the time you are hearing this. Instead of worrying about percentage of intake, determine your ideal weight and then make sure you consume one gram of protein for each pound of ideal body weight you are striving toward. This is the recommended amount for active people whose ranks you are, hopefully, about to join. If you take up bodybuilding or start running marathons, you may need more. You need protein for everything from muscle to immune system antibodies. Many brain chemicals are also made from the amino acids you get from protein. Foods such as milk, cheese, eggs, poultry, red meat, and fish are good sources of protein. That's why I always take high protein energy bars with me when training for long distance kayak and cycling trips. I also take some that are high in carbohydrates when I need a quick energy boost.

Different Types of Carbohydrates. Carbohydrates contain four calories per gram and are the main energy source for the body. When three or more 6-carbon sugar molecules are joined, the resulting molecule is known as a complex carbohydrate. One or two 6-carbon sugar molecules linked together comprise a simple sugar. Complex carbohydrates are further classified into fibrous and starchy carbohydrates. When consumed, simple sugars, like sucrose and dextrose, as well as refined complex carbohydrates, like white flour, provide a burst of energy that often gives way to feelings of lethargy. Typically, unrefined complex carbohydrates are assimilated by the system more slowly than simple sugars and will provide constant and sustained (though less intense) energy levels.

Limit Sugars in Favor of Low Glycemic Index Carbohydrates. The lower the glycemic index of a given carbohydrate, the more gradually it will be digested into its component parts and absorbed from the GI tract into the bloodstream. Less insulin is released from the pancreas over a given time in response to foods with low glycemic indices. Hence, the body has more time to utilize the molecules for fuel, rather than storing them as fat.

Consume Adequate Fiber. Because the human gastrointestinal (GI) tract cannot digest fiber, it does not contribute calories and is passed as waste. It is, nonetheless, vital to good health. Inadequate dietary fiber leads to a sluggish GI tract, water retention, bloating, constipation, and an increased risk of developing colon cancer. In addition to being rich in vitamins, minerals, and antioxidants, fruits and leafy vegetables are excellent fiber sources, and most experts advise consuming at least five servings per day. For optimal fat burning, limit starchy carbohydrate consumption later in the day, eating plenty of fresh fruits and vegetables, instead.

Eat a Low-Fat Diet. Fats contain 9 calories per gram, more than twice the amount found in carbohydrates and proteins. Saturated fats, derived from animal sources, have been shown to contribute more heavily to the development of cardiovascular disease than unsaturated fats, derived from plant sources. For health reasons, fats should be limited to less than 20% of total, consumed calories.

Drink A Lot of Water. Many nutritionists recommend that the active individual consume a minimum of one gallon of water per day, although that will vary depending upon your level of activity and the weather. Water aids the liver and kidneys in the detoxification of toxins and in the elimination of wastes from the body. Without sufficient water, we become dehydrated, and our organs (including muscle, liver, and kidney) do not function optimally. Optimal kidney function leaves the liver free to perform maximum lypolysis, or fat burning. In addition, water is both an appetite suppressant as well as an excellent diuretic. Not only will high fluid intake increase urination, it also will decrease overall water retention. Although you may have to work up to a gallon a day gradually over a week or so while your bladder adjusts, you will reap the benefits of your efforts almost immediately. In fact, drinking water below your body temperature can actually help you to lose weight. Did you know that consuming one gallon of water chilled to 4 degrees Fahrenheit could cause your body to liberate over 150 calories of energy? What an easy way to burn fat! Of course if you are running low on energy, this practice could, theoretically, make you even more lethargic, but probably not as much as the extra weight you are carrying. Therefore, I wouldn't be concerned about this issue. Be careful. Too much water can dilute your electrolytes and result in heart failure. There are lots of recommendations regarding the amount of fluid you should consume. For some people it may be close to a gallon per day. For others, it may be less. Let the sensation of thirst and the color of your urine be your guide. The sensation of thirst indicates you are not consuming enough. Urine that is darker than a light, straw color is sending the same message. You need enough and that is likely to vary from one person to another. Check with a Registered Dietician if you are not sure.

Aim to Prevent, Not Quench, Your Thirst. Proper hydration leads to enhanced thermo-regulation and increased oxygen exchange in the lungs. Simply stated, the well-hydrated individual will have greater endurance and a more comfortable workout. Since we do not feel thirsty until we are already in a dehydrated state, it is best to drink water with sufficient frequency to prevent thirst.

Eliminate Alcohol. Alcohol is not exactly classified as a nutrient, but it is widely consumed and warrants mention. Alcohol is the enemy of the dieter and the athlete. It contains 7 calories per gram, nearly as much as fat, and is completely without nutritional value. Not only does alcohol contribute empty calories, it slows the body's metabolic rate so that fewer calories are burned over time. In addition, alcohol consumption leads to a transient hypoglycemic state and subsequent food cravings. Finally, alcohol is hepatotoxic, and even moderate drinking can result in fatty deposits on the liver. When the liver works hard to detoxify the system of alcohol, it is less efficient at lipolysis, or fat burning.

Keep Track. Use a book or other guide to keep track of your total calorie consumption as well the proportion of carbohydrates, protein, and fat you consume. You should measure your food (with a measuring cup or scale) until you have a good idea of exactly what a portion actually represents. Most people overestimate portion size and, hence, underestimate their caloric intake.

Emotions:
Ally and Enemy

Emotions are the link between your beliefs and how you conduct your life. They impact your immune system and memory as well as your cardiovascular and endocrine systems. Even your reaction time and ability to perform are associated with emotions. Emotions can impede your progress or motivate you to achieve new heights. For instance, sadness can preoccupy you, or it can prompt you to change your circumstances. Fear may paralyze you, or it can prompt you to take precautionary steps, which, in turn, may save your life. Emotions are a double-edged sword. Without them, your life would be dull and meaningless. But too much of a good thing, especially at the wrong time, can derail you.

What Are Emotions?

First and foremost, you should recognize that *emotions are really nothing more than a sensory system. They are*

the eyes and ears of your body . . . gauges of your biology.
The brain is a huge endocrine gland that secretes behavior and emotions. The emotions and behavior that are excreted have a biological basis. But it's not like putting a dipstick into the motor of your car to see what the oil level happens to be. You can't put your finger in your ear or up your nose, and then look at it to measure the amount of acetylcholine, norepinephrine, or serotonin in your brain. More often than not, the negative emotions reflect the perception of unmet needs; there is a problem which gives rise to anger or fear. But it's very important to realize that the emotion itself is not the problem. Emotions are nothing more than symptoms or indicators of a problem. Many people make the mistake of believing that the emotion is the problem. They go to the bookstore and purchase a volume proclaiming to have the solution for vanquishing their anger or for reducing their fear. That's all well and good. By all means, take steps to reduce the anger or the fear that impedes your productivity or blocks your capacity for pleasure. However, at the same time, recognize that if all you do is put a pharmacological or behavioral Band-Aid on the emotion, the problem that led to that emotion will resurface at some other time, perhaps in the form of a derailed immune system, or, possibly, in the form of intestinal upset, skin disease, memory loss, or heart problems. There are a wide number of illnesses that will more readily occur when your body has been altered by emotional upheaval. Imagine how difficult it would be to achieve goals if you had to cope with all these emotion associated maladies.

There are no fewer than 558 words in just the English language that have emotional connotation. Of course, that gets a bit unwieldy. In contrast, the British philosopher John Locke argued that there are really only two emotions: those that give rise to pain and those that give rise to pleasure. The negative emotions are those that are associated with a threat or with the blocking of a goal. The positive emotions, on the other hand, are associated with making progress toward a goal. Is it that simple? Are emotions just good or bad? Is it really that clear-cut? What do you believe? The ancient Greeks would have argued that all emotions are good; that the ability to express virtually every emotion is essential for the good life. A counterpoint was promoted by the Stoics, who argued that it was a waste of time to experience emotions, especially joy and love, which were considered frivolous. And you can't blame them. Life was absolutely chaotic during that era in ancient history. It really was a waste of time to be joyful because there were few sources of pleasure. The belief that emotions are inherently bad was driven home during the Middle Ages. Realize that at that time, they didn't use the word *emotion*. Instead, the word *passion* was used and was very closely intertwined with sin, focusing on words like *greed*, *lust*, and *envy*. To this day, this historical perspective has influenced our cultural beliefs concerning emotions. Despite evidence to the contrary, emotions often are believed to be inherently bad, which may be why many people deny or repress them.

You've heard the expressions—you've probably used them yourself: *Don't be so emotional. Chill out. Be more reasonable.* The implication is that emotions are the opposite of reason; that if you express the emotions that you have, somehow, you have lost control. Not only is this a cultural belief; it often is a hand-me-down belief, as well. It may well explain the reluctance of some people, especially men in Western society, to express their feelings. Why do some people avoid emotions? People do things for one of two reasons: to avoid pain or to experience pleasure. If a child has a traumatic experience as a result of being punished for expressing anger, she will associate anger with pain, and it will be avoided. If a boy is brought up in an environment where he is taught that the male is the one who always should be strong and in charge, the experience and expression of fear may erode that self-image. So the emotion and the circumstances that might give rise to it are avoided. In many instances, if you are uncomfortable with the expression of a certain emotion, you may very well align yourself with an individual who also feels uncomfortable with expressing the same emotion. Whether in the workplace or in the family, you reinforce each other and behave in a way that each of you feels comfortable with by avoiding the same emotion.

In other cases, opposites may attract. You may be drawn to a person who is able to express an emotion that you feel uncomfortable with because it makes you feel complete. In other words, opposites both attract and repel, depending upon the circumstances. It can end up being a very stable relationship, but it also has the potential to be very dull and boring, especially when implied mutual consent banishes certain emotions from the relationship. A few years ago, I was asked to present a lecture on the subject *The Power of Positive Emotions*. It was only a 30-minute talk. But I spent more time working on that 30-minute lecture than I often put into a multi-day program for a large corporation. And there were two reasons for this: the person presenting before me was Richard Simmons, and the person coming on stage immediately after me was Naomi Judd. I was well aware that nobody cared about me. I had been hired by the organizers of a large health fair to bridge the gap between the light-hearted, 'fun' presentation of Simmons, cavorting about the stage in his pink and white shorts and tank top, and the very serious, spiritual message of Naomi Judd. The organizers estimated that it would take about 30 minutes to change the set—and my job was to keep the audience entertained in the meantime.

Actually, that was not really the problem. That was a challenge and, I might add, fun to tackle. The real difficulty was trying to decide which emotions belonged in the positive column and which in the negative column. I couldn't figure it out. Oh, I read the same books you've probably read, but I couldn't agree with the authors. And then one morning when I was out riding my bicycle, I had one of those 'Aha' moments. It suddenly dawned on me that there is no such thing as a positive emotion. All emotions are negative. And then I realized that there are no negative emotions. They are all positive. It is not the emotion that is positive or negative. It is the context in which it arises. It is the match between the emotion and the circumstance that determines whether the same emotion can have survival value or whether it will be impede your ability to achieve goals. Let's consider a couple of examples.

Anger is very often placed in the negative column, which it most certainly is when that anger is repressed, or when the anger, which should be expressed to a co-worker or supervisor in the work-place, is taken home and misdirected at your children or your spouse. Yes, that anger is then a very negative emotion. But, if you use anger to motivate you to identify the underlying, unmet need or problem, and, if you express anger in an appropriate way, that anger becomes a virtue, not a vice. Conversely, the emotion of love is routinely placed in the positive column, which it most certainly is when directed at your children, parents, or your spouse. But, when that same emotion of love is now directed at the spouse of your next-door neighbor, it becomes a very negative, destructive emotion. So is the expression of love that you find depicted in many Valentine's Day cards, the ones that proclaim, *"I couldn't live without you." "I love you so much that my life would not be complete if you were not a part of it."* This, I believe, is a very sick, co-dependent type of love, which fails to provide the individuals in the relationship the opportunity to grow. If you delve into history and literature, you discover that what happened to Romeo and Juliet was the rule, not the exception. That kind of dependent love gets people imprisoned in castles, run over by trains, and murdered—that's if they don't commit suicide first. The same is true of your beliefs.

There is no such thing as a good or bad belief. It is only when a belief is not justified under a particular set of circumstances that it becomes bad. So, like the emotions that they can give rise to, it is the match between a belief and the environment that has to be examined. Even though beliefs and emotions are distinct entities, realize that the belief gives rise to an emotion, which, in turn, communicates through chemicals with the rest of the body. Thus, when you change a belief, it will most likely evoke simultaneous changes in your emotional well-being, your body chemistry, and your health. Through the examination of your beliefs, you can take control and make progress toward achieving your dreams. You can also take steps to directly lessen the impact emotions have upon your well being. Here are seven options to keep emotions from sapping your will to press on toward a goal.

Seven Ways to Deal with Emotional Turmoil

1. Translate your emotions into language. Talk out loud or simply write the problem down. This will enable you to view the problem through a different sensory modality, for example, the auditory or visual system, giving you a different perspective from which to identify causes and/or solutions.

2. Identify the emotion you are experiencing. Are you feeling sad, angry, fearful, guilty, embarrassed, or a combination of these or others?

3. Identify the source of the problematic emotion. Are you angry with yourself for not accomplish-

ing a goal? Are you fearful or sad about the consequences for not having done so? Are you feeling guilty because you failed? And remember that what really causes you to blow up at the end of the day may very well be some event you've been mulling over all day long.

4. Identify the negative thoughts you might be experiencing and hold them up to reality.

5. Identify those thoughts, which are grossly exaggerated and replace them with more rational thoughts. For example, if you happen to be late for a family gathering, don't assume your family will think that you don't love them. Recognize that they will probably accept that your tardiness was due to reasons outside your control.

6. Re-think the entire scenario. Just as a result of going through the steps at this point, you probably have already avoided a major, emotional crisis.

7. Once you figure out what went wrong, take corrective action. Learn from your mistakes, and set about to make sure it doesn't happen again. Remember that even your biggest blunder can always serve as a bad example for future choices.

When Panic Attacks

There are some individuals who experience very intense, physiological symptoms that will occur repeatedly and quite unexpectedly in the absence of any apparent, external trigger. These are referred to as panic attacks, and they are thought to occur when the body's normal stress circuitry becomes inappropriately aroused. Some or all of the following symptoms may accompany these episodes. There may be an impending fear of dying, a concern about totally losing physical or emotional control, going crazy, or doing something embarrassing. Some people lose their sense of reality, experience flushes or chills, and/or tingling or numbness in the hands. Other individuals experience difficulty breathing, dizziness, chest pains, as well as a racing or pounding heartbeat. Perhaps the best way to describe these attacks is with the word 'terror.' There is a sense that something unimaginably horrible is about to occur and the person experiencing it has no power to prevent it.

So severe are these attacks that, in many individuals, it is the anxiety associated with the possibility of having another panic attack that, in turn, serves as a trigger for emotional upheaval. The initial panic attack may often be associated with some form of stress, such as fear or failure that a goal may not be achieved. It may result from being overworked, or it may be secondary to the loss of a close family member or friend. Some people experience the attacks following the stress associated with surgery, a serious accident, illness, or even childbirth. Certain drugs also can stimulate panic attacks, for example, excessive consumption of caffeine or the use of cocaine can sometimes trigger these types of reactions. Despite the association with stress, these attacks usually take people totally by surprise, and it is their unpredictable nature that results in their being so disruptive.

Obviously, a preoccupation with such disruptive events will stifle any motivation to proceed toward a goal. Here are several strategies for coping with panic, and these will be worthwhile, whether the panic attacks occur intermittently or on a regular basis.

- It is important to remember that, although they may seem to be overwhelming, your feelings are not, by themselves, dangerous or harmful.

- Know that if you are experiencing a panic attack, you are experiencing the very same physiological changes that evolved to enable you to survive an emergency. You are simply experiencing an exaggeration of your normal response to stress.

- Don't try to force the feelings away. The more you are willing to recognize the feelings and face them head-on, the less intense they will become.

- Avoid exacerbating your attack by dwelling on what might happen now or in the future.

- Maintain a constant flow of calming and affirming self-talk. Remind yourself that you are in no real, physical danger; that you've gotten through this before, and you will survive it again; that the physical symptoms will pass, and it is safe to relax.

- Breathe, slowly and deeply, from your diaphragm. This promotes the relaxation response in the body, as well as serves as evidence that you are, indeed, able to breathe just fine.

- You might try quantifying your level of fear. Assign a number from 1 to 5, with 5 corresponding to the most intense feelings of fear that you might experience and 1 being minimal intensity. Then rate yourself. What you will observe is that your feelings of anxiety do not remain constant. Instead, they fluctuate. And they'll stay at a very high level for only a few seconds at a time.

- Distract yourself. Shifting your attention to a repetitive task may divert your attention and your anxiety.

By utilizing these strategies, you will notice that when you stop engaging in behaviors that add to your fear, the anxiety itself will begin to fade away. You also will become instantly aware that these strategies do work, and this will make you feel good about the fact that you have succeeded and by exerting a degree of control over the situation. Once you acquire this understanding, you will be ready to successfully achieve your goals.

Overcoming Fear

It's now time to learn some skills to help you better handle self destructive emotions. Many people cling to outmoded beliefs because they enable them to avoid an emotion that causes pain or discomfort. For example, *Complaining gets you nowhere.* Let's imagine that this belief has its roots in early childhood when a complaint triggered a belligerent reaction on the part of a parent. (For example, Dad believed children should be seen and not heard.) Yes, in that environment and at that time, the child's belief was justified. It kept the kid out of trouble in the home. The fear response elicited by the parent's angry outburst had definite survival value. But, things have changed. In the retail store, it's not healthy to internalize anger because you still believe it's wrong to complain about having been overcharged. Or to simply fume over the overcooked steak at the restaurant and say nothing to the waiter. All you've done is replace the fear associated with speaking out with the anger of feeling wronged. Simply registering a complaint could so easily have dissipated that anger. I'll bet that if you really were to think about it, there are many things that you regret not having done out of fear. Even within the past 24 hours, you may well have stretched *turn the other cheek* beyond its intended boundary.

The first question to ask is, *"Is this belief that it's wrong to complain justified?"* The answer is *No*. There's nothing noble about being wronged and saying nothing. When you have been overcharged for a purchase, the belief that it is wrong to speak up is not justified. *"Is the belief serving a useful purpose?"* Of course not. It's serving a harmful purpose. Doing nothing is one of the behaviors normally associated with a feeling of helplessness, a feeling that will erode your health faster than anything else.

Let's approach change by starting with the end. After all, it would require a great deal of time and the skills of a gifted therapist to travel back in time and revisit your early childhood to identify the possible cause of the belief. Instead, let's start at the end with the fear that you are trying to avoid. When you cast aside all the details, what you are left with is a belief that enables you to avoid the emotion of fear. That's what you can fix.

At Saddlebrook Resort, I have created a program designed to deal with what is probably the greatest impediment to personal growth and success: the fear of failure. I focus upon the issue of fear at the outset by taking them out of their comfort zone, away from all the things that provide security. They are taken into the woods where there are no walls displaying certificates of achievement; where there's no place for the coat and tie they rely upon to convey power and authority in the workplace; where the expensive gold watch or reserve of cash are of no value. That alone enables some people to push their personal comfort envelope and learn to deal with the mild fear of being in a novel environment. Of course, everyone is having fun building camaraderie during the process. There's no reason why learning a valuable lesson cannot be enjoyable. And, sometimes, this serves as a useful diversion, or what I referred to elsewhere in this program as emotional interference. The friendly exchanges, as people enter this unfamiliar territory, serve to counterbalance their uncertainty.

In this new environment, the old, familiar beliefs are easier to let go of as a new group with a different purpose and different dynamics begins to form, a group that now requires different skills to function effectively. This is the first critical step to change—getting rid of old, unhealthy beliefs and conditioned habits. In this new environment, the ability to predict has vanished, giving rise to uncertainty. The five acre course includes suspension bridges high in the trees, a zip line, countless problem-solving initiatives, and a 40 foot rock-climbing wall. There are also two telephone poles. One task requires they climb the pole and then jump off in an attempt to hit a ball suspended high above them. Some people greet this new environment and the uncertainty it brings with excitement and even elation. Others clearly are uncomfortable being away from their normal routine. In his or her own way, each person is dealing with change on their terms. I have created an environment where they can learn to overcome fear safely. The stock-boy with rock-climbing experience overcomes his nervousness of speaking to the owner of the company when it becomes clear to the group that his skills now are going to be a tremendous asset. And the CEO learns to deal with the discomfort of being in a subservient position and having little to offer in this new setting. No one is ever pressured into crossing out of their comfort zone. But, if they want to explore, one small step at a time, what it's like to experience a fear response and then recovery from it, they can do it safely, in a wonderfully supportive environment. That evening, they hear an after-dinner talk, using film clips of the day's activities, during which I discuss many of the issues I'm now delving into.

When it's over, people are better equipped to deal with the fears of change. They have learned to accept change and to cope with uncertainty on their terms so that when they experience similar challenges in the workplace or in their personal lives, they can do what my family does after an adventure vacation. The body can shrug off any new challenge by saying, *"Been there, done that, and got the tee-shirt, no problem."* Bring on the next challenge. I call it Cross-Stressing. It's analogous to a child acquiring a new language. Learning a foreign language is very difficult. But, once it's acquired, it becomes relatively easy to acquire another new language because the child has a learning set for languages. What you can do is acquire a learning set for change and coping with adversity. The ability to face the emotional consequences of change head-on will enable you to accept the risks you have to take to establish new boundaries in your professional and personal life.

If you cannot accept change, you will always remain where you are now. That is not to bring about success in a world that is in a constant state of flux. This concept applies not just to the business world, but to your relationships, as well. A healthy business organization is a living system, constantly in the process of growing. Individuals who have the capacity to deal with change drive healthy companies. Healthy people also recognize that during the course of a relationship, they and their partner change. Healthy people are willing to constantly examine their beliefs as they prepare for inevitable change in both their personal and professional lives. But you cannot learn to change without accepting some potential risk, if nothing else, the prospect of failure. The training itself can be risky as you face your beliefs head-on and set about to create new mental images to better match your ever-changing circumstances. Here's an exercise that I call *Pushing Your Emotional Envelope.*

Beginning today, I want you to practice dealing with change and the emotion of fear. For the next week, do one thing each day that is a departure from your normal way of behaving. It doesn't matter what it is. The only objective is to familiarize yourself with the feeling. And I'm not suggesting that you take up a dangerous sport or throw yourself in harm's way. There are many things that you can do that are quite safe from a physical standpoint, but which provide the opportunity to grow emotionally. Do you have a fear of public speaking? Then attend a PTA or city council meeting and make it a point to stand up and comment about an issue. Do the same at your next company training session. Ultimately, you might volunteer to make a presentation at a fundraiser or join a church choir. Is winning your objective? Even on the highway, where you always want to be in front of the car ahead? Or, first off the line at the traffic light? Then ease off on the accelerator, and be a follower. Let another motorist move ahead of you so that you can experience the emotion you have been trying to avoid. Are you always in control and the expert in your organization? Then become a volunteer. Spend some time at a homeless shelter, serving food or sweeping floors. Offer to help do something, knowing in advance that you have limited skills in this arena. Step out of your comfort zone, and learn to accept advice and instruction from others.

I once enrolled in a 5-day training program on how to run a ropes course. It was a new experience for me.

For years, I'd been the person in front of the classroom, presenting the training and being asked the questions by medical students. Suddenly, I found myself immersed in a group of people half my age and with largely physical education backgrounds, not science. No one had any need for my information, and I had few answers to the questions being posed. Instead, I was doing the asking, while seeking the skills I eventually would need. I was a stranger in this environment. Even the frost during that fall in Massachusetts was a departure from the warmth I had grown accustomed to at my home in Florida. But, the experience gave me new insights about other aspects of my life. Just experiencing the feeling associated with that unfamiliar role provided me with a different way of looking at things.

There's another way you can teach yourself to better handle negative emotions—experience them on your terms and discover that they really aren't all that bad. When I conduct multi-day training programs, I will give participants an assignment to find a partner and do something that's legal and reasonably safe, but which takes them outside their emotional comfort zone. The reason I have them pair up is because there's safety in numbers, plus the other person provides the extra motivation that is sometimes needed. Remember, we each have a finite amount of motivation. When more than one person teams up, their combined motivation can be shared. It makes it easier to achieve the goal. Here are some of the things people have done during these training sessions:

- Approach a stranger
- Cut in front of a long taxi line
- Swim in a public fountain
- Ride a roller coaster
- Gamble
- Hold a snake
- Go skinny dipping
- Eat unappealing food
- Sky dive
- Rock climb
- Argue with a friend
- Parasail
- Speak in public
- Wear outlandish clothes/makeup
- Bungee jump
- Climb a radio antenna
- Swim in cold water
- Jump off a high-diving platform
- Go to the top of a tall building
- Confess a weakness to an admirer
- Say no when expected to say yes
- Ride on a motorcycle

Some of these things may be a part of your normal routine and therefore, not all that stressful. However, for some individuals, these activities may offer an opportunity to experience what emotional discomfort can be like. More importantly, they got over it. That's the key element. Successfully recovering from adversity is how we learn to be optimistic. *"This, too, shall pass"* is the lesson learned. And if it's really bad, from that point on, you can reflect upon the experience, and when confronted with a different type of challenge, say to yourself, *"I'm glad I'm not* _____ *"* (in cold water, bungee jumping, or whatever you did that raised your adrenalin).

Use successive approximation. Take small steps until you feel comfortable leaving your familiar surroundings and operating with a new set of beliefs. Examine each emotion that you experience along with your beliefs. By immersing yourself in novel environments, you'll develop the ability to accept and trust others, and to gain the confidence to accept change. Armed with those skills, there is no limit to what you will achieve. Accepting the challenge to achieve a goal has no guarantee of success. Indeed, failure could result in some rather undesirable outcomes, as well as missed opportunities while in pursuit of the goal.

I once was faced with that same dilemma soon after graduating from the University of Florida Medical School. I'd been offered a very good job at the University of Texas Medical School in Galveston. It was a tenure-track position, which, even in those days, was difficult to secure. At the same time, I was offered a position with the National Geographic Society to lead an expedition to study whales in the West Indies. I did all of the things you're supposed to do: I sought input from trusted academic advisors. One said, *"Nick, if you go down to the West Indies, you will be committing academic suicide. You'll never keep up; you'll forget everything you learned. Don't throw away your education."* And other people said the same thing. That's when I created two lists; one included all of the reasons why I should have accepted the job at the medical school in Texas, and I filled up a legal pad. And then I made a list of all of the reasons why I should go to the West Indies, and I could have fitted them onto a postage stamp.

But then I re-framed the question. Instead of asking myself, *"What should I do?"* I asked, *"What will I regret not having done at some future date?"* And within weeks, my wife and I packed up our then six-month-old daughter and sailed off into the sunset. To this day, I have never had a real job, and, at this stage in my life, I probably never will. Did I make the right decision? I don't know. There's no way of ever knowing, so I don't even bother to ponder the matter. Do I have any regrets? Absolutely not. I've accumulated a treasure chest of experiences and, in the process, learned to adapt to just about every category of change. So, while you are thinking of reasons not to do the things you can and should, take a moment to step out of the present, and peer into the future. That new perspective may be just the vantage point that you need to make the right choice. There's one more thing. You are converting one of the most powerful emotions you ever experience into a catalyst for change. Fear of regret is now replacing fear of failure. Instead of a fear holding you back, you now have converted it into a force to propel you forward.

Take Control
Over Your Life

By posing questions and examining your beliefs, you have begun to take control. No, not control over other people, but control over yourself. Many people believe they have no choice but to relinquish control to others, especially under duress. They become embroiled in an altercation with their supervisor and then adopt the attitude that, *"There's nothing I can do. If I say anything or do anything, it won't make any difference, and I'll probably lose my job."* They believe they are helpless. This can wreak havoc upon the body. A very important belief to have is that you can do something. I'll briefly review three studies to illustrate just what I mean.

- First, experiments have revealed that when laboratory animals are stressed, if they are able to press a bar and turn the stressor off, this control will offset some of the health problems that would arise if they lacked this control. In short, it is not the stressor that causes the health problems, but the belief that they have no control over it.

- Second, if the animals have had control, and then the bar is disconnected, they still do better than those that never had any control. This is because they believe things are still better. They still experience the stress after pressing the bar, but based upon the previous experience, they perceive things are not as bad.

- Third, a large group of animals was given 10 stressors an hour. The day before, half had received 20 shocks, and half received just one. Who suffered the most, even though the stressor is now identical for both groups? It was the group that previously received just one. Why? Because going from 20 stressors to 10 instills a sense of optimism that things are getting better, while those animals that went from 1 to 10 have nothing to be optimistic about; for them, things are getting worse.

These, and many other, well-controlled studies, clearly reveal that the belief that we are in control, even in the absence of any benefit, coupled with the belief that things are improving, are sufficient to not only lessen the stress response, but to reduce the probability of developing stress-related illnesses. However, be careful with this concept of control. Too much control can be just as detrimental to your health as too little. This was revealed through studies in Vietnam. Investigators found that it was middle management, or the middle-level officers, who had to make a lot of very important decisions affecting the lives of many men under their command, who suffered most from the effects of stress, as compared to those troops who simply followed orders and went out into the rice paddies. So, having too much control—or too much responsibility—also can be detrimental to your health.

But, being completely helpless is also a serious problem. That is why I strongly recommend that you always do something in an adverse situation, even if the probability of a positive outcome is very remote. What is important is that you not act like a victim. So often when a person is in the midst of an altercation, especially in the workplace, they will shrug their shoulders, walk away from the problem, and adopt the attitude that, *"There is nothing I can do. If I say anything or do anything, I will probably be put on the night shift for the rest of my life."* Or, *"I'll never get another day off. I might even lose my job."* So they walk down to the coffee pot, and they talk about the person behind his back, which is not necessarily a bad thing. It's when you internalize an emotion that it wreaks havoc on your immune system and on your overall health. But if that's all you do, it's going to be extremely detrimental to your health. When you walk away with the attitude that there is nothing you can do, you are acting like a victim, thereby, making your belief a self-fulfilling prophecy. If all you do is talk about the person, you will fuel your emotion without addressing the problem that gave rise to it. Ultimately, it will be detrimental not only to the person you are talking about, but to yourself as well.

While it's okay to talk about the situation, it's preferable to do it with the person who has triggered your response. It may turn out that doing nothing is the best thing to do. But if you do nothing, make sure it is because you choose this as one of several options. Don't do *nothing* because you believe that your hands are tied and that there are no other choices. Sometimes, doing nothing is, indeed, the best choice to make. But make sure that you give yourself a metaphorical bar to press.

However, it is not always this simple. The fact is *one size does not fit all.* There are some people who believe that they must have complete control and responsibility over as many things in their environment as possible. And then there are other people who believe that it is best for someone else to do it all. There is nothing wrong with either belief. Problems arise when people who want responsibility and control are in situations where this desired responsibility and control are not available. Or, when people who feel more comfortable having someone else make the decisions are suddenly put in the driver's seat. Once again, the problem is a mismatch between people's beliefs and their environment. Additional conflict may arise because people change. You are not the same person under stress that you are when all is calm. Under pressure, you may become just the opposite of what you usually are. Most of the time, people will adhere to the belief that they developed in their family unit, so if they were encouraged to be inquisitive, or to argue, that's probably the way they'll be the rest of their lives. If they were encouraged to be silent and not to speak up, that will be their tendency. Then people will seek out employment and environments where there is a match between the ways they are comfortable responding and what they have to do. Under stress, however, the rules change. The same people who want control in times of calm may become acquiescing or accommodating under stress. On the other hand, people who have been accommodators will now suddenly seize the reins of control. But because this type of response is not one they are accustomed to experiencing, this lack of familiarity may give rise to yet another source of conflict. Realize that the critical variable of control is not a simple one.

Actually, I'm not even sure if *control* itself should be the objective. Instead, it needs to be viewed as a process for achieving closure. Of course, you are more likely to experience closure when you are in control. At the same time, I think it is all right for someone else to have that control as long as the person giving it up is comfortable with the arrangement. There are some people who, obviously, cannot completely control their medical circumstances, but they trust in their doctor or other healthcare provider. The belief that the doctor is in control and will make the right decision can be just as good in achieving closure. So can a belief in a higher power—believing that what is happening to me right now is part of some large, unified plan—and that there is, ultimately, going to be a beneficial outcome. You don't have to know what that outcome will be, or what direction things are going to go. But whether they get worse or whether they get better, the belief that this is part of some large plan and that there will, eventually, be closure can help some people deal with turmoil.

When All Else Fails

Sometimes you simply can't control circumstances. The environment might have failed so rapidly that there's nothing you can do about it. And you may have very limited control over your physical or behavioral responses. You may be paralyzed—perhaps with fear. But there is always one thing you do have control over right up until your dying breath, and that is your attitude, which no one can take away from you. You cannot really control another person's behavior, nor can they control what you do. Granted, it may be extremely difficult to control your responses to another person's actions. But, ultimately, that control resides within you via your attitude, and it just may save your life.

I have a very good friend whose life was saved because of his attitude. He just retired as a special agent in charge of a tactical training program at the FBI Academy. We have worked together creating adventure programs at Saddlebrook Resort for corporate clients who want to learn how to overcome fear. In the late 1960's, Phil was in Vietnam as part of a special unit that was ambushed by the enemy. Everyone in the unit was killed, except Phil, who should have died. He was hit 13 times with bullets from AK47 machine guns. But, he survived against all medical odds. I once asked him why? Why he was able to overcome such medical odds. He replied, *"While I was lying on the ground unable to move, feeling the life literally drain out of me, I was absolutely determined that I was going to stay awake so when the enemy came over to slit my throat or put a bullet in my head, I was going to spit in their faces and glare at them so that they would know that I was dying on my terms and not on theirs."* Well, it turned out that none of the enemy had survived the encounter. There was no one left to slit his throat, so not knowing this, he remained awake until, eventually, an evacuation helicopter arrived.

That is exactly the type of fighting spirit that Dr. Bernie Segal writes and lectures about, a spirit that characterizes individuals who do not accept the belief of others. When they are told that the odds of surviving the cancer are very remote, they reply by saying, *"My body doesn't know about statistics. I am not average. I'm going to be the exception."* They are the people who take control. They fight until the bitter end, and often they overcome seemingly insurmountable odds, just as Victor Frankel did when he was incarcerated in the Nazi concentration camps. He was once asked why it was he survived when so many others died from starvation, disease, and torture. His answer was eloquent in its simplicity, *"The belief that one day I would be asked that question."* He was able to see beyond the barbed wire, as he remained optimistic that there would be life after the camp. In addition, he seized control over those things in his life that he could influence. There was much he wasn't able to control; but, by ritualizing the act of brushing his teeth in the morning and by making a big production of getting dressed, he seized control over the small things in his environment that he was able to influence. He never surrendered his spirit to that feeling of total helplessness. No one sprinkles you with magical dust to induce a belief that you can't do something. No one presses a button on the side of your head that induces an emotion. These are your responses, and no one can ever control them for you. No one. In the end, the very belief, 'You are in control,' may save your life. It may also enable you to endure one of the greatest fears we have in Western society, which is the fear of dying. If having control and a sense of optimism can help a person overcome one of the greatest fears known, you can rest assured that the same principles could work wonders in helping you to overcome the fear of failure that might arise during the pursuit of a goal.

Personality and Goals

I'm sure that you've heard of the so-called Type A personality, the person who is always in a hurry, who never takes time out to smell the roses, who often speaks rapidly, and who finishes your sentences for you because he gets impatient waiting for you to finish saying whatever it is you're going to say, probably because whatever you have to say is not important to him in the first place. There is a certain amount of overlap between the Type

A personality and what is referred to as the *controlling personality*. This person is basically in a win/lose mode. *"I'm going to win; you're going to lose. We are going to do it my way, or we are not going to do it at all."* This person is often threatened by dialogue. If you disagree with him, he'll take it as a personal affront. *"Why waste time talking about the problem? We're going to do it my way, anyway, so let's just get on with it."*

You've probably heard that it is the time-oriented, controlling personality who is most likely to succumb to a heart attack. Well, that's only partially correct. That was the interpretation of the data from the Framingham Heart Study when first completed. And on the basis of the limited information available to the psychologists at that time, that was the correct interpretation. But, it was only a correlation. Subsequently, Dr. Redford Williams and others designed more expansive studies. It turns out that they discovered there was something else that accounted for most of the correlations between the Type A personality and coronary arterial disease. Anger and hostility, the emotions of stress, were largely responsible. In other words, it's all right to be a workaholic, just don't be an angry, hostile workaholic. And if you are, for heaven's sake, don't internalize it. That makes things even worse.

Let's consider next the so-called Type C personality. This is the person who is the opposite of the controller, one you would call the accommodator. This person is in a lose/win mode. *"I'm going to lose; you're going to win. Your needs are more important than mine. There's no point in talking about this since we're going to do it your way, any-way."* This is the person Lydia Temoshok labeled as the Type C or cancer-prone personality. This is the person George Solomon described as being susceptible to rheumatoid arthritis. This is a very passive individual, one who will experience a great deal of personal discomfort in order to please other people. Evidence suggests that they have a difficult time dealing with negative emotions, especially in others. In a clinical setting, this person will wait until his throat is parched before troubling the staff for a glass of water. Then he will apologize for having taken the staffs' time. He is just the opposite of that Type A on the second floor, the one who constantly is demanding the nurses' time, wanting to know, *"Why am I taking this pill and that pill, and what do you mean waking me at 2 o'clock in the morning to give me a sleeping pill?"* He is the person who in the clinical setting is often labeled as difficult to manage. It's no surprise that's the person who does not get much voluntary attention. Yet, despite this, the demanding person is the one who is most likely going to survive, whereas the passive, sweet individual is likely to experience a worse outcome.

Reflect for just a moment on these two personalities, but from the standpoint of control. The person asking the questions would not do so if he did not believe that there were going to be an outcome. In other words, he has made himself a part of the negotiation of his treatment. He has given himself a metaphorical bar to press. In contrast, the Type C individual has basically abdicated responsibility, handing it over to the healthcare provider. *"Here I am. Do whatever you will."* Oh, I'm sure that there are many factors and explanations as to why one person has a better prognosis than another. But, in view of the data that I briefly summarized a little while ago, there is no question in my mind that giving up control is a very important variable. Acting like a victim is never healthy. There's another personality type that you hear about, which is the so-called Type T or Thrill Seeking personality. These are people who take calculated risks and include bungee jumpers, skydivers, and motorcycle racers. It is the Type T individual who does not accept conventional wisdom or certain existing beliefs. This is a person who explores new horizons and who is always looking for a different way to do things. This is the person who makes discoveries and who is not afraid of risk, indeed, who thrives on it. It doesn't hurt to have at least a small amount of Type-T in your makeup. After all, doing something different, even if it's positive, carries the inherent risk of failure. An unwillingness to take such risks may be what's holding you back.

There are other personalities as well. For example, there's the collaborator, who is in a win/win mode. *"I want to win, but I'm concerned about your needs. I want you to win as well."* This person is very different from the controller. Collaborators are energized by disagreement. They welcome dialogue. There are also avoiders, who are the corporate equivalent of repressors. *"Problem? What problem?"* These same people fail to acknowledge unmet needs within their own body, just as they neglect important issues in the workplace.

These are just a few of the designations used to describe personality types. I want you to realize that there is nothing wrong with any of them. Just like beliefs, it is not the personality that is good or bad, but the context in which it is exhibited. Thank goodness all of our mothers were, at least temporarily, Type C's. Thank goodness they were willing to sacrifice their own need for sleep in order to nurture us as infants. We would never have survived if they had not been willing to do that. In that environment, being a Type C is a beneficial response. It is not good, however, when you are recovering in a hospital bed, and you place other people's needs ahead of your own—not when you are the one who needs the nurturing. You might believe the collaborator is the best way to be, and it, most certainly, is in many environments, especially the business environment. When I'm lecturing to corporate clients, that is exactly what I encourage them to be like. The focus used to be on always winning. Now, a more collaborative stance is advocated for many work environments. Organizations recognize that even their competitors play a useful role in the economic ecosystem.

But there are times when being the collaborator is not the best way to be. If you happen to be a law enforcement agent staring down a criminal's gun, that is not the time to be asking, *"Look, I really want to know what your needs are. How about I just cuff one of your hands, would that be all right?"* In law enforcement, coming in second is not good enough. Winning is everything, just as it is in the healthcare setting. When you are the person who has been diagnosed with cancer, you don't want your doctor coming up to you and saying, *"Look, there is a treatment for which you are an ideal candidate, and it's practically guaranteed to put your cancer into remission. The problem is it is still considered by some insurance companies, including yours, as being experimental, so they won't pay for it. But that's okay. There's another treatment. It's not as good, although there's still an 80 percent chance you'll survive by using that treatment."* You are not going to accept that kind of collaboration. There is only one option in that circumstance, and that is the best and the most effective treatment. If the insurance doesn't cover it, you expect the doctor to be your advocate and figure out a way to get you into that experimental protocol.

For everything, there is a season. That includes your personality—or, rather, your personalities. You see, we are really each composites of these different personalities. I hope you don't interact with your children in the same way that you interact with your coworkers. I hope you don't treat your spouse in the way that you treat subordinates at work. I hope your personality does vary depending upon the circumstance. And for that reason, I wish we could dispense with the label 'personality' altogether because it's really a coping style. Problems arise when the coping style or personality displayed is inappropriate for the environment. And when does that happen? When your beliefs give rise to mental images that fail to accurately depict reality. If you want to achieve the goals you know you can, but you just don't, realize that you need a healthy mix of several personalities.

Printed in the USA
CPSIA information can be obtained
at www.ICGtesting.com
JSHW012036140824
68134JS00033B/3085